MW00895382

Contents

Listen and repeat. Then act out.

	Subject Pronouns	Object Pronouns
Singular	I You He She It	Me You Him Her It
Plural	We You They	Us You Them

1 Write *he*, *she*, *it* or *they*.

1 ....*it*....

2 ....

3 ....

4 ....

5 ....

6 ....

7 ....

8 ....

2 Complete the sentences.

1 **Mike** is ten years old.	.... is ten years old.
2 **Tim and I** are friends.	.... are friends.
3 **Elena** is a teacher.	.... is a teacher.
4 **The house** is old.	.... is old.
5 **Cara and Pedro** are from Spain.	.... are from Spain.
6 **The boys** are in the kitchen.	.... are in the kitchen.

3 Read and underline the correct word.

1 You're hungry. Here's a cake for <u>you</u> / me!

2 They're nice flowers. Let's draw it / **them**!

3 I'm funny! Look at **me** / us!

4 Mark is a good singer. Listen to you / **him**!

5 The tigers are scary. Look at us / **them**!

6 You and Lisa are dirty. Look at you / **us**!

7 It's a ball! Catch me / **it**!

8 Emma is pretty. Look at him / **her**!

The verb 'to be'

Affirmative		Negative	
Long form	Short form	Long form	Short form
I am	I'm	I am not	I'm not
You are	You're	You are not	You aren't
He is	He's	He is not	He isn't
She is	She's	She is not	She isn't
It is	It's	It is not	It isn't
We are	We're	We are not	We aren't
You are	You're	You are not	You aren't
They are	They're	They are not	They aren't

4 Complete the sentences.

— Long Form —

1 They *are* in the garden.
2 She .... at home.
3 We .... happy.
4 I .... hungry.

5 He *is not* at home.
6 I .... thirsty.
7 Ann .... a doctor.
8 She .... in the room.
9 They .... English.

— Short Form —

They *'re* in the garden.
She .... at home.
We .... happy.
I .... hungry.

He *isn't* at home.
I .... thirsty.
Ann .... a doctor.
She .... in the room.
They .... English.

Personal Pronouns – 'Be' – 'Have (got)' – 'Can'

Interrogative	Short answers	
Am I?		
Are you?	Am I / Are you tall?	Yes, I am.
Is he?		No, I'm not.
Is she?		
Is it?	Is he/she/it in the garden?	Yes, he/she/it is.
Are we?		No, he/she/it isn't.
Are you?	Are we/you/they students?	Yes, we/you/they are.
Are they?		No, we/you/they aren't.

5 **Put the words in the correct order to make sentences as in the example:**

1 I – years – eight – old. – am
   I am eight years old.

2 you – England – from – are?

3 they – sisters – aren't

4 a – is – he – student

5 in – they – garden – the – are?

6 my – in – class – isn't – she

6 **Write am, is or are.**

Hello, I 1) ......*am*...... Nick and this 2) ....
Peter. We 3) .... friends. Peter 4) ....
nine and I 5) .... ten. Peter and I 6) ....
from London. We 7) .... students at Park School.

7 **Complete the questions. Then read again and answer them.**

1 ...*Are*... Nick and Peter brothers? ....
2 .... Peter nine? ....
3 .... Nick nine, too? ....
4 .... Peter and Nick from London? ....
5 .... Peter and Nick singers? ....

8 Ask and answer. Then write.

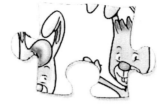

1 .... *Is* .... it a flower?   2 .... they ducks?   3 .... it a kite?

Yes, ... *it is* .... .   No, ...   No, ...

4 .... he a clown?   5 .... she a teacher?   6 .... they birds?

Yes, ...   No, ...   Yes, ...

What am I?

GAME

What animal are you? Talk with your friend and find out.

Student 1: Am I a cat?
Student 2: No, you aren't.
Student 1: Am I a duck?
Student 2: Yes, you are. My turn now!

The verb 'have got'

Affirmative		Negative		Interrogative
Long form	**Short form**	**Long form**	**Short form**	
I have got	I've got	I have not got	I haven't got	Have I got?
You have got	You've got	You have not got	You haven't got	Have you got?
He has got	He's got	He has not got	He hasn't got	Has he got?
She has got	She's got	She has not got	She hasn't got	Has she got?
It has got	It's got	It has not got	It hasn't got	Has it got?
We have got	We've got	We have not got	We haven't got	Have we got?
You have got	You've got	You have not got	You haven't got	Have you got?
They have got	They've got	They have not got	They haven't got	Have they got?

9 Put the words in the correct order to make sentences as in the example:

1 three / I've / hats / got
I've got three hats.

2 a / we've / big / got / house
....

3 coat / got / a / pink / she's
....

4 old / he's / an / watch / got
....

5 I've / new / toothbrush / got / a
....

6 got / computer / have / you / a?
....

7 three / got / brothers / hasn't / he
....

8 teacher / we / a / new / haven't / got
....

9 car / haven't / a / we / got
....

10 a / she's / dress / got / red
....

Short answers

Have you got a car?	Yes, I/we have.	No, I/we haven't.
Has he/she/it got a car?	Yes, he/she / it has.	No, he/she/it hasn't.
Have they got a car?	Yes, they have.	No, they haven't.

10 Look at the pictures and write questions and answers.

1 .Has it got .... small ears?
.No, it hasn't.............

2 .... long tails?
....

3 .... big feet?
....

4 .... short hair?
....

5 .... a small nose?
....

11 Complete the email with *am*, *is*, *are*, *have got* or *has got*.

◀▶ C +

Dear Kelly,

　　Hi! How 1) *are* you? How 2) .... your new school?

　　I 3) .... in Year Six at school now. I 4) .... a new teacher, Mr Finns.

He 5) .... 38 years old and he 6) .... quite tall. He 7) .... fair

hair and glasses.

Sam 8) .... a new computer and Roy 9) .... a new bike. It 10) ....

really cool! Guess what! I 11) .... a pet dog, Sparks.

　　12) .... you .... any new friends in Moscow? Write and tell me.

Love,

Amy

12 Complete the questions. Then read the email again and answer them.

1　*Has* .. Amy ... *got* ..... a new teacher?　..................................
2　............... Mr Finns .... dark hair?　..................................
3　............... Sam .... a new computer?　..................................
4　............... Sam and Roy .... a new bike?　..................................
5　............... Amy .... a pet dog?　..................................

Never-ending Game

Say what you've got. Your friend repeats what you say and adds what he/she's got.

Student 1: I've got a cat.
Student 2: He's got a cat and I've got a fish.
Student 3: She's got a fish and I've got a duck, etc.

The verb 'can'

Affirmative	Negative		Interrogative
	Long form	Short form	
I can	I cannot	I can't	Can I?
You can	You cannot	You can't	Can you?
He can	He cannot	He can't	Can he?
She can	She cannot	She can't	Can she?
It can	It cannot	It can't	Can it?
We can	We cannot	We can't	Can we?
You can	You cannot	You can't	Can you?
They can	They cannot	They can't	Can they?

13 **Look at the picture and write.**

1 Ian ....*can ride a horse*.......... .   5 Sue ....

2 Fatimah ....*can't ride a horse*.... .   6 Juan ....

3 Mary ....   7 Jim ....

4 Ahmed ....   8 Carmen ....

14 Put the words in the correct order to make sentences as in the example:

1 can / I / ride / bike / a
I can ride a bike.

2 can / really / swim / Tina / well

3 football / can / they / play

4 a / my / can / brother / car / drive

5 hands / clap / can / your / you?

6 can't / horse / ride / a / I

15 Answer the questions.

1 Can you stamp your feet? .... *Yes, I can.* ....
2 Can you make a sandwich? ....
3 Can your grandfather climb a tree? ....
4 Can you jump over tall trees? ....
5 Can you stand on one leg? ....
6 Can you walk like a monkey? ....
7 Can your grandma make a banana cake? ....

3 Listen and repeat. Then act out.

We use Can I ...? to ask for permission when we want to do something.

16 Complete the questions and answers.

1 .... *Can I* .... go to the cinema?   No, *you can't.* ....
2 .... use your computer?   No, ...
3 .... have some more pie?   Yes, ...
4 .... buy some comics?   Yes, ...

17 Read and match.

1 Can I watch TV?
2 Can I go to the park?
3 Can I make the biscuits?
4 Can I buy some sweets?
5 Can I go swimming?
6 Can I eat your sandwich?
7 Can I have your pencil?

a Yes, you can. Your towel is in your wardrobe.
b No, you can't. It's very late.
c Yes, you can. Here it is.
d Yes, you can. I'm not hungry.
e No, you can't. It's very cold outside.
f No, you can't. They're bad for your teeth.
g Yes, you can. The eggs are in the fridge.

Brain GYM

You've got three minutes. Read and answer.

1 Can you write the next three numbers?   2, 4, 6, ...
2 Can you write three types of clothes beginning with 's'?   . . . .
3 Can you write three school subjects?   . . . .
4 Can you write three food items beginning with 'c'?   . . . .
5 Can you write four animals with four legs?   . . . .

Speaking Activity

How well do you know your friend? Answer the questions. Check your answers with your friend.

1 What is your friend's name?   3 What does he/she look like?
2 How old is he/she?   4 What can he/she do well? (e.g. dance, etc.)

Writing Activity

Write about your friend.

My Friend . . . .
by . . . .
My friend . . . . is . . . . years old. . . . .
has got . . . .
. . . . can . . . .
. . . . My friend is great fun!

Plurals – This / These – That / Those

 Listen and repeat.

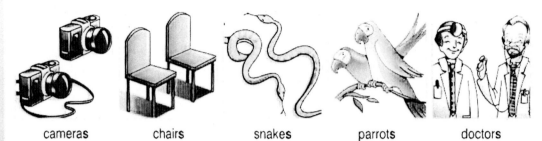

cameras   chairs   snakes   parrots   doctors

We form the plural of most nouns by adding 's'.

1 Look at the pictures. Write the plurals.

1 one apple   two *apples*.   2 one bird   two . . . .   3 one shoe   two . . . .

4 one dolphin   two . . . .   5 one clown   two . . . .   6 one spider   two . . . .

2 Write in the plural.

1 It is a bird.
   They're birds. . . . .

2 He's a clown.

   . . . .

3 You've got a friend.

   . . . .

4 Look at the bat.

5 She is a doctor.

6 Look at the shark.

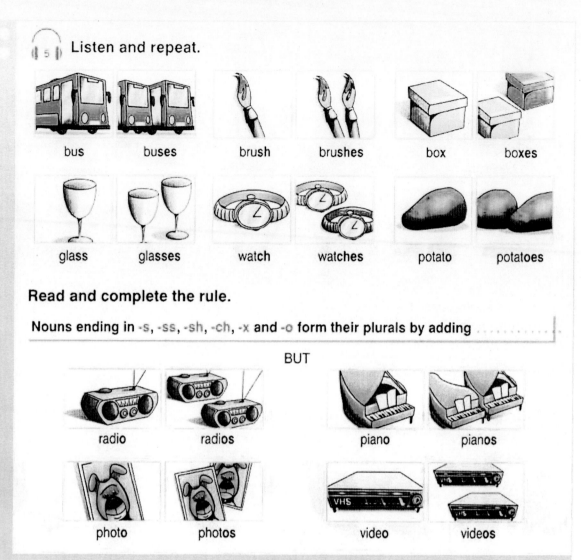

🎧 **Listen and repeat.**

bus — buses brush — brushes box — boxes
glass — glasses watch — watches potato — potatoes

Read and complete the rule.

Nouns ending in -s, -ss, -sh, -ch, -x and -o form their plurals by adding ....

BUT

radio — radios piano — pianos
photo — photos video — videos

---

3 Look at the pictures. Write the plurals.

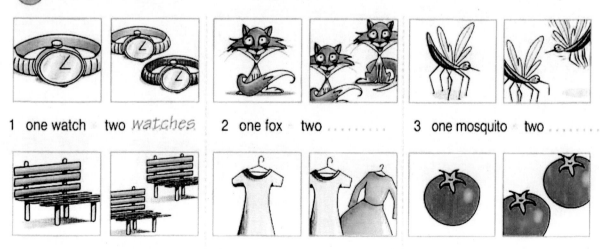

1 one watch   two *watches*   2 one fox   two ....   3 one mosquito   two ....

4 one bench   two ....   5 one dress   two ....   6 one tomato   two ....

Listen and repeat.

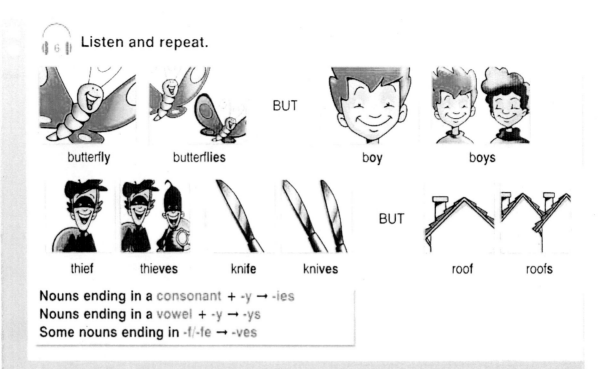

butterfly   butterflies   BUT   boy   boys

thief   thieves   knife   knives   BUT   roof   roofs

Nouns ending in a consonant + -y → -ies
Nouns ending in a vowel + -y → -ys
Some nouns ending in -f/-fe → -ves

4 Look at the pictures. Write the plurals.

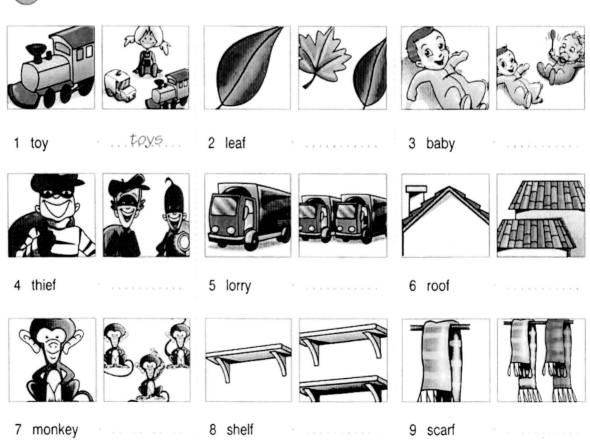

1 toy   ...toys...   2 leaf   ....   3 baby   ....

4 thief   ....   5 lorry   ....   6 roof   ....

7 monkey   ....   8 shelf   ....   9 scarf   ....

5 Write the plurals in the correct columns. Listen and check. Listen and repeat.

| banana | knife | butterfly | tomato | leaf | class | toy | wolf |
| sandwich | lady | baby | bus | spider | scarf | piano | fly |

–s	–es	–ies	–ves
bananas			

Irregular Plurals

Listen and repeat.

tooth – **teeth**

foot – **feet**

goose – **geese**

man – **men**

woman – **women**

child – **children**

sheep – **sheep**

fish – **fish**

deer – **deer**

mouse – **mice**

ox – **oxen**

6 Write the plurals.

1 a pen – two   *pens*   7 an ox – four
2 a bus – ten   8 a deer – two
3 a woman – two   9 a child – two
4 a mouse – three   10 a class – three
5 a fish – three   11 a foot – two
6 a tooth – five   12 a sheep – ten

7 Match. Then write the plurals.

carrot	tomato
apple	pumpkin
cherry	knife
sandwich	cake

1 six *tomatoes*
2 four
3 seven
4 nine
5 eight
6 two
7 three
8 five

An adjective describes a noun.
It is an **old** book. (What kind of a book is it? It's **old**.)

Adjectives remain the same in the plural.
They are **old** books. (NOT: They're ~~olds~~ books.)

Remember: We use a/an only in the singular form.

---

8 Write in the plural.

1 It's a funny film.
   They're funny films.

2 He's a tall man.

3 She's a good teacher.

4 Look at the black sheep.

5 I'm a nice girl.

6 It's a pretty baby.

Plurals – This / These – That / Those

Some nouns are uncountable. They have no plural. These are:

bread	money	cola	juice	wood
lemonade	cheese	water	sugar	milk
butter	tea	jam	meat	paper
chocolate	coffee			

Note: A/An is not used with uncountable nouns. Some is used instead.
We say: a carrot   BUT   some bread

9 Circle the correct item.

1 a / **an** apple
2 a / **some** chocolate
3 a / **some** sandwich
4 a / **an** banana

5 a / **some** coffee
6 a / **some** potato
7 **an** / **some** sugar
8 a / **an** olive

9 a / **some** lemon
10 **an** / **some** onion
11 a / **an** strawberry
12 a / **some** jam

10 Look at the pictures. Write *a*, *an* or *some*.

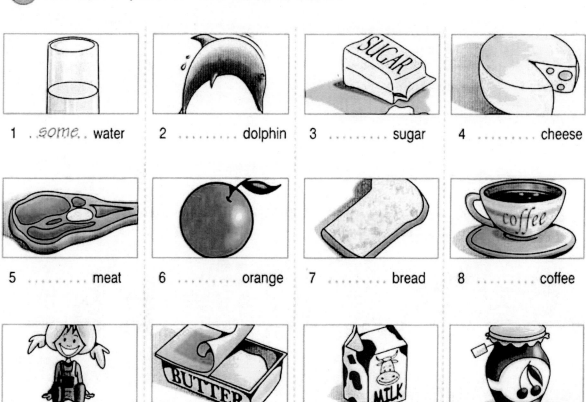

1 . *some* . water
2 .... dolphin
3 .... sugar
4 .... cheese

5 .... meat
6 .... orange
7 .... bread
8 .... coffee

9 .... doll
10 .... butter
11 .... milk
12 .... jam

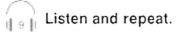 Listen and repeat.

| a **bottle** of milk | a **glass** of water | a **cup** of tea | a **loaf** of bread | a **slice** of bread | a **box** of cereal |

| a **jar** of honey | a **can** of cola | a **piece** of cheese | a **bowl** of soup | a **carton** of milk | a **kilo** of butter |

Uncountable nouns can be made countable by using the above words.
some tea – a **cup** of tea

11 Look at the pictures. Write the correct words.

 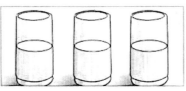 

1 two ..*bowls*.. of soup   2 three .... of water   3 two .... of bread

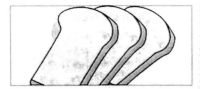  

4 three .... of bread   5 two .... of lemon juice   6 two .... of milk

7 two .... of cake   8 three .... of cereal   9 three .... of cola

  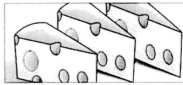

10 two .... of coffee   11 three .... of jam   12 three .... of cheese

12 Circle the odd one out.

1 a bag / (carton) / kilo of sugar   4 a bottle / glass / box of water   7 a glass / carton / jar of juice

2 a cup / jar / slice of coffee   5 a slice / glass / loaf of bread   8 a piece / box / kilo of cheese

3 a glass / kilo / bottle of cola   6 a piece / kilo / loaf of meat   9 a jar / can / slice of honey

13 Choose the correct word and complete the sentences. Then act out.

1 A: Can I have a _cup_ (cup, piece, carton) of tea, please?
  B: Here you are.

2 A: Here are three _____ (jars, cans, pieces) of cake, all for you.
  B: Thank you, Grandma. You're so kind.

3 A: Can you buy a _____ (bottle, box, kilo) of milk, please?
  B: Sure.

4 A: We need a _____ (bowl, kilo, box) of meat.
  B: OK.

5 A: Can I have a _____ (carton, kilo, glass) of water, please?
  B: Yes, of course.

Spot the Differences

GAME In pairs/groups, spot six differences. The winner is the pair/group who finds all the differences first.

Student: In picture A, I can see one dog. In picture B, I can see ... , etc.

This / These – That / Those

🎧 10 **Listen and repeat.**

This is my pet.

That is my kite.

These are my pets.

Those are our kites.

We use this and these when we talk about people, animals or things that are near us.

We use that and those when we talk about people, animals or things that are far from us.

14 **Read and circle.**

1 **This / (That)** is a watch.

2 **These / Those** are strawberries.

3 **This / These** is a goose.

4 **Those / That** are mice.

5 **This / That** is a bowl of soup.

15 Write *This*, *That*, *These* or *Those*.

1 ....*This*.... is a coconut.

2 .... are jars of jam.

3 .... is an orange.

4 .... is a carton of milk.

5 .... are tomatoes.

6 .... is a slice of bread.

7 .... are watermelons.

8 .... is a jar of honey.

9 .... is a lemon.

10 .... are limes.

16 Write sentences.

(cat/horses)

1   *This is a cat.*
2   *Those are horses.*

(cake/presents)

3   ....
4   ....

(toy/helicopters)

5   ....
6   ....

(computer/books)

7   ....
8   ....

(flowers/trees)

9   ....
10 ....

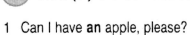

(cat/lions)

11 ....
12 ....

17 Tick (✓) the correct sentences. Correct the wrong ones.

1   Can I have **an** apple, please?   ✓
2   Can you buy **a** bread, please?   *some*
3   Can you draw **a** picture for me?   ....
4   Can I have **a** mouse as a pet?   ....
5   Can I buy **a** new dress?

6   Can I have **a** milk, please?   ....
7   Can I buy **a** skirt?   ....
8   How much is **these** hat?
9   I like those **sheeps**.
10 Can you buy a **box** of milk?

Speaking Activity

You are a famous chef. Make your own dish. Give it a name. What is there in it? Tell your friend.

My favourite dish is Super Soup. All you need is five carrots, two onions, three potatoes and some meat. Delicious!

Writing Activity

Write about your favourite dish.

.... (name of dish)

by ....

My favourite dish is ....

....

....

....

1 **Choose the correct item.**

1 Mary and I .... sisters.
  (A) are   B am   C is

2 .... you play tennis?
  A Can   B Have   C Are

3 I .... got a new computer.
  A can't   B am not   C haven't

4 They've got three ....
  A child   B children   C childs

5 Look at the baby's .... They're so big.
  A foots   B foot   C feet

6 Who are .... ?
  A they   B him   C them

7 Where is Anna? I can't see .... !
  A her   B she   C he

8 The story is about a man and two ....
  A foxes   B fox   C foxies

2 **Complete the sentences.**

1 *This* is my *bike* .

2 *Those* are *buses* .

3 .... are my ....

4 .... is a ....

5 .... are ....

6 .... are my ....

3 **Underline the correct word.**

I've got four 1) **leg / legs**. I 2) **has / have** got a long tail, too. I've got very big 3) **tooth / teeth**. I 4) **am / can** swim but I can't climb 5) **tree / trees**. My favourite food is 6) **meat / meats** and fish. You can sometimes see me at a zoo. What 7) **are / am** I? I'm an alligator.

Listening

4 🎧 11 Listen and draw lines. There is one example.

5 🎧 12

We've got lots of food to eat
These are apples
That is meat
We've got lots of food to eat
It's dinner time

We can make a tasty dish
This is butter
Those are fish
We can make a tasty dish
It's dinner time

You can have some food with me
Those are burgers
That is tea
You can have some food with me
It's dinner time

25

Possessives

🎧 **Listen and repeat. Then act out.**

Possessive Adjectives (followed by nouns)	Possessive Pronouns (not followed by nouns)
my	mine
your	yours
his/her/its	his/hers/ –
our	ours
your	yours
their	theirs

1 Complete the sentences. Then write the children's names.

1 I am Fred. ... *My* ... hair is short and red.
2 **He** is Ivan. .... eyes are green.
3 **She** is Maya. .... hair is long and dark.
4 **We** are Tom and Claire. .... hair is short and fair.
5 **They** are Bruce and Jill. .... eyes are blue.

Fred

2 Complete the sentences with the correct possessive pronoun.

1 **Mike** has got a computer. It's   *his*   .
2 **I** have got a rabbit. It's   .
3 **Karen** has got a new sweater. It's   .

4 **We** have got a new house. It's   .
5 **You** have got a brown coat. It's   .
6 **They** have got a big flat. It's   .

3 Complete the sentences with the words in the list.

his	her	hers	your	yours	my
mine	our	ours	its	their	theirs

1 I'm Becky. This is .... *my* .... rabbit.
2 This is Juan and this is .... sister.
3 The boys have got comics. The comics are
   ....
4 We're in .... garden today.
5 Look at Nadia and Khalid. They're in
   .... car.
6 Lisa has got a bag. The bag is ....

7 I'm Adam. That bike is ....
8 We're hungry. These sandwiches are
   ....
9 You and Ben are brothers. Ben is ....
   brother.
10 Isabel hasn't got .... book today.
11 That bird is funny. Look at .... tail!
12 Hello, Amy. Is this hat .... ?

Possessive Case with people

 Listen and repeat.

the boy's hat

the girls' skirts

We use 's with one person.   **We use s' with two or more people.**

BUT   the children's books, the women's bags, the men's umbrellas

Note: We also use 's with animals. the cat's tail

Read and complete the rule.

Whose skirt is it? It's **Linda's**.
We use .... to ask about who owns something.

4 Look at the pictures and write.

1 This is *Mary's umbrella.*
  It's *her umbrella.*
  This *umbrella is hers.*

2 These are . . . .
  . . . .
  They're . . . .
  These . . . .

3 These are . . . .
  . . . .
  They're . . . .
  These . . . .

5 Answer the questions.

Isabel   Ben   Tom   Elisha   Jenny   Youssef

1 Whose camera is it?
  It's Tom's camera.

2 Whose flowers are they?

3 Whose ball is it?

4 Whose cars are they?

5 Whose ice cream is it?

6 Whose books are they?

Possessive Case with things

We use of with things.

the trunk of the tree

6 Look at the pictures and write sentences.

1 **(car/roof)** *Where's the roof of my car* .... ?

2 **(house/door)** Where's .... ?

3 **(bike/wheels)** Where are .... ?

4 **(clock/hands)** Where are .... ?

Who's Mike? = **Who is** Mike?   BUT   **Whose** hat is it? It's Mike's.

7 Write *Who's* or *Whose*.

1 "..*Who's*.... Mike?" "He's my brother."

2 "............ bike is it?" "It's mine."

3 "............ jacket is this?" "It's Emma's."

4 "............ that man?" "I don't know."

5 "............ Cara?" "She's my sister."

6 "............ radio is it?" "It's my friend's."

Feely Bag

Whose is it? Each of you puts an item (e.g. a pencil, an eraser, etc.) in a bag. Take an item out and try to guess whose it is.

Student 1:   It's Kelly's pencil.

Kelly: Yes, it's mine. My turn now.

Possessives

8 Underline the correct word. Then find three mistakes in the picture.

This is 1) **I / <u>my</u>** new cartoon character. 2) **He's / His** name is Spot. 3) **His / He's** got fair hair and blue eyes. 4) **Spot's / Spots'** favourite food is chocolate cake. 5) **Her / His** favourite music is rap and he likes tennis. Spot is from the planet Sitcom. 6) **Their / His** mother and father are there. 7) **Their / They're** names are Sparks and Specks. Spot's friend on earth is a girl. 8) **His / Her** name is Martha. Martha and Spot have a lot of fun together!

Speaking Activity

Think of a new cartoon character. Answer the questions. Talk with your friend.

1 What's the name of your new cartoon character?
2 What's his / her favourite colour / food / music / sport?
3 Has he / she got a family? What are their names?
4 Has he / she got a good friend? What's his / her name?

Writing Activity

Write about your new cartoon character.

This is my new cartoon character. . . . . name is . . . .

. . . .

. . . .

🎧 15 **Listen and repeat.**

In Choco Town, there's a baker's and a bank. There are two sweet shops but there aren't any trees.

	Affirmative		Negative		Interrogative
	Long form	**Short form**	**Long form**	**Short form**	
Singular	There is	There's	There is not	There isn't	Is there?
Plural	There are		There are not	There aren't	Are there?

1️⃣ **Look at the map and complete the sentences.**

1 ....*There's*........ a hospital in ....*Hallam*........ Street.

2 .... two cafés in .... Street.

3 .... a library in .... Street.

4 .... a theatre in .... Street.

5 .... a bus stop in .... Street.

2️⃣ **Complete the questions. Then look at the map again and answer them.**

1 ...*Is there*... a hospital in Hallam Street? ....*Yes, there is.*........

2 .... a bank in Quick Street? ....

3 .... two theatres in Hallam Street? ....

4 .... two cafés in Quick Street? ....

There is / There are – Some / Any

3 Look at the picture. Fill in: *There is, There are*.

1 ..*There are*.. two swings in the garden.
2 .... a slide.
3 .... two children.
4 .... two chairs.

5 .... two cats.
6 .... four birds.
7 .... a ball.
8 .... a table.

● Memory game!

Teacher: *Is there a slide in the garden?*
Team A S1: *Yes, there is.*

4 Answer the questions.

1 Is there a TV in the classroom?
   Yes, there is. ....

2 Are there six chairs in the classroom?
   ....

3 Is there a teacher in the classroom?

4 Is there one window in the classroom?
   ....

5 Is there one book in the classroom?
   ....

6 Is there a fish in the classroom?

5 Look at the picture and write questions and answers.

1 three children?
   Are there three children?
   No, there aren't. There are six.

2 a birthday cake?

3 one bottle of cola?

4 five glasses?

5 five lollipops?

6 one present?

 Listen and repeat.

There isn't any cheese. There aren't any bananas. There isn't any jam. But there's some bread. Here, have some.

some / any

some + countable **or** uncountable nouns (in affirmative sentences)	any + countable **or** uncountable nouns (in questions and negative sentences)
There are **some** tomatoes. There is **some** bread.	Are there **any** oranges? Is there **any** milk? No, there isn't **any** milk.

6 Look at the picture and write sentences.

- carrots
- chocolate
- meat
- potatoes
- cola
- pineapples
- cheese
- bananas
- flour

1 *There are some carrots.*
2 *There isn't any chocolate.*
3
4
5
6
7
8
9

7 Write *some* or *any*.

1 There are *some* potatoes in the bag.
2 Are there .... eggs on the table?
3 There is .... sugar in the bowl.
4 Is there .... butter in the fridge?
5 There is .... cola in the bottle.
6 Are there .... chairs in the room?
7 There aren't .... books on the shelf.
8 Is there .... meat in the shop?

8 Look at the picture and write questions and answers.

1 apples? *Are there any apples?*
   Yes, there are.
2 eggs?
3 butter?
4 tomatoes?
5 milk?
6 oranges?
7 meat?

Mind Reading

Guess which picture your friend is thinking about.

PICTURE A

PICTURE B

Student 1: Are there any strawberries?
Student 2: Yes, there are.
Student 1: Is there any chicken?
Student 2: Yes, there is.
Student 1: It's Picture B!

Writing Activity

Write about the two pictures.

In Picture A, there are ....

....

....

....

In Picture B, there are ....

....

....

....

1 Circle the correct item.

1 This book is **my** / **mine.**
2 Mr Smith is **their** / **theirs** teacher.
3 This is **our** / **ours** house.
4 **My** / **Mine** cat is black and white.
5 This is **Marks** / **Mark's** car. It's very fast.

6 The black skirt is **her** / **hers**.
7 This is John's book. It is **his** / **her**.
8 This car is **their** / **theirs**.
9 Dr Black is **her** / **hers** doctor.
10 My **friends** / **friend's** flat is very small.

2 Look at the picture and write questions and answers.

1 *Are there any* pictures?
   Yes, there are.
2 *Is there* a table?
   No, there isn't.
3 .... a phone?

4 .... books?

5 .... flowers?

6 .... chairs?

7 .... a bed?

8 .... a cat?

Listening

3 17 **Listen and tick (✓) the box.**

1 What's in the basket?

A ☐   B ☐   C ✓

3 What's on the table?

A ☐   B ☐   C ☐

2 Whose baby brother is he?

A ☐   B ☐   C ☐

4 Whose bag is it?

A ☐   B ☐   C ☐

4 18  Song

This is my rubber
It's mine, mine, mine
Mine, mine, mine
Mine, mine, mine
This is my rubber
It's mine, mine, mine
I can go to school

Those are his books
They're his, his, his
His, his, his
His, his, his
Those are his books
They're his, his, his
He can go to school

This is her pen
It's hers, hers, hers
Hers, hers, hers
Hers, hers, hers
This is her pen
It's hers, hers, hers
She can go to school

These are our bags
They're ours, ours, ours
Ours, ours, ours
Ours, ours, ours
These are our bags
They're ours, ours, ours
We can go to school

5

🎧 19 Listen and repeat.

He is reading a newspaper. She is bringing the salad. The children are fighting. The cat is eating the chicken.

Affirmative		Negative	
Long form	**Short form**	**Long form**	**Short form**
I am working	I'm working	I am not working	I'm not working
You are working	You're working	You are not working	You aren't working
He is working	He's working	He is not working	He isn't working
She is working	She's working	She is not working	She isn't working
It is working	It's working	It is not working	It isn't working
We are working	We're working	We are not working	We aren't working
You are working	You're working	You are not working	You aren't working
They are working	They're working	They are not working	They aren't working

We use the present continuous for actions happening now.

Spelling

work – work**ing**   open – open**ing**   play – play**ing**   walk – walk**ing**

BUT

danc**e** – danc**ing**   run – run**ning**   li**e** – **ly**ing

How do we form the present continuous? Choose.

A subject + be (**am, is, are**) + verb -ing
B subject + be (**am, is, are**) + verb

1 Add *-ing* to the verbs.

1 walk	.....*walking*.....	5 give	....	9 tell	....
2 read	....	6 sit	....	10 go	....
3 swim	....	7 open	....	11 dig	....
4 eat	....	8 close	....	12 finish	....

2 Circle the correct item.

1 Jenny **is** / **are** helping her mum now.
2 You **am** / **are** visiting your grandma at the moment.
3 The girls **am** / **are** having breakfast at present.
4 My dad **is** / **are** sleeping on the sofa.
5 We **is** / **are** walking to school now.

6 I **am** / **are** doing my homework.
7 It **is** / **are** raining today.
8 Our mum **is** / **are** cooking dinner.
9 The birds **am** / **are** singing.
10 My friends **is** / **are** playing tennis at the moment.

3 Write the sentences in the negative.

1 I'm reading a book.
   I'm not reading a book.

2 Bill is playing a computer game.
   . . . .

3 The boy is running.
   . . . .

4 Your dad is driving his car.
   . . . .

5 We're watching TV.
   . . . .

6 The boys are writing in their notebooks.
   . . . .

7 It's snowing now.
   . . . .

8 Helen is laughing at the moment.
   . . . .

4 Look at the pictures. Match and write sentences.

☐1 **Grandpa / sleep**
☐ **Fatimah / listen to music**
☐ **Anna and José / cook**

☐ **Sally / cry**
☐ **Jane and Nora / dance**
☐ **Father / dig in the garden**

1 *Grandpa is sleeping.*　　2 . . . .　　3 . . . .

4 . . . .　　5 . . . .　　6 . . . .

Present Continuous

5 Put the words in the correct order to make sentences as in the example:

1 playing / he's / violin / the
   He's playing the violin.

2 school / going / we're / to

3 aren't / they / the / playing / in / park

4 me / aren't / listening / you / to

5 playing / is / he / the / guitar

6 isn't / he / sleeping

6 Circle five differences. Write sentences.

In picture B ...

1 *Mike isn't playing the violin. He's playing the guitar.*

2 ....

3 ....

4 ....

5 ....

Interrogative	Questions	Short answers
Am I working?	**Are you** working?	Yes, I am.
Are you working?		No, I'm not.
Is he working?	**Is he/she/it** working?	Yes, he/she/it is.
Is she working?		No, he/she/it isn't.
Is it working?		
Are we working?	**Are they** working?	Yes, they are.
Are you working?		No, they aren't.
Are they working?		

7 Answer the questions.

1 Is he sleeping?
Yes, he is.

2 Is she driving?

3 Is it running?

4 Are you sending an email?

5 Are they listening to music?

6 Is he playing the piano?

8 Write the questions and answers.

1 he / eat / a cake
Is he eating
a cake?
No, he isn't.
He's eating a burger.

2 they / play / with a kite
?

3 he / drive / a car
?

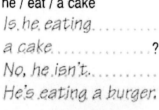  

4 she / pick / flowers
?

5 they / sing
?

6 she / cook / chicken
?

We usually use the following time expressions with the present continuous: now, at the moment, at present, today. We also use the following imperatives with the present continuous: Look! Listen!

9 Fill in the correct form of the verbs. Circle the time expressions and imperatives.

It's winter but it 1) ..*isn't snowing*. **(not/snow)** (today) The children 2) . . . . **(not/ play)** in the house now. They're in the garden. At the moment, Ben 3) . . . . **(not/ride)** his bike. He 4) . . . . **(throw)** snowballs! The girls 5) . . . . **(make)** a snowman. Look! The girls 6) . . . . **(not/wear)** their scarves. Their scarves are on the snowman! Can you see Mum? Listen! She 7) . . . . **(sing)**!

Let's mime!

Mime an action. Your friends try to guess what you're doing.

Student 1: What am I doing?
Student 2: Are you playing basketball?
Student 1: Yes, I am. Your turn now.

10 Fill in the correct form of the verbs. Then find Mark in the picture.

Dear Mum,

We 1) ..*are having*.. (have) lovely weather today. The sun 2) ....

.... (shine). I 3) ....

.... (wear) my favourite T-shirt and shorts. Ahmed and I 4) ....

(sit) under trees. We 5) ....

.... (eat) ice cream and we 6) .... (listen) to music!

I love this place!

Love,

Mark

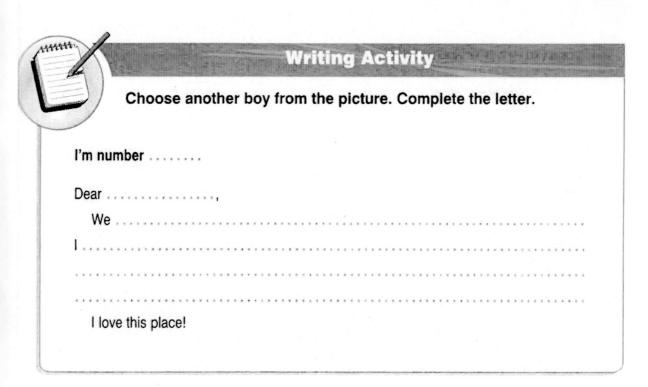

Mark is number ......

Writing Activity

Choose another boy from the picture. Complete the letter.

I'm number ....

Dear ....,

We ....

I ....

....

....

I love this place!

Present Simple

(| 20 |) Listen and repeat.

Mary, Mary, quite contrary
How does your garden grow?
I feed the bees, I water the trees,
And I plant my potatoes in a row.

Affirmative	Negative	
	Long form	**Short form**
I work	I do not work	I don't work
You work	You do not work	You don't work
He works	He does not work	He doesn't work
She works	She does not work	She doesn't work
It works	It does not work	It doesn't work
We work	We do not work	We don't work
You work	You do not work	You don't work
They work	They do not work	They don't work

Read the rhyme and tick (✓).

1 Mary **feeds** the dog.
Yes, she does. ☐
No, she doesn't. ☐

2 She **waters** the trees.
Yes, she does. ☐
No, she doesn't. ☐

Spelling

I work – he work**s**   I sing – he sing**s**

BUT

Verbs ending in -ss, -sh, -ch, -x, -o → -es	**Verbs ending in** consonant + -y → -ies
I wash – he wash**es** I go – he go**es**	I cry – he cr**ies** BUT I play – he play**s**

We use the present simple for permanent actions, routines and repeated actions.

Time Expressions with Present Simple

once a week, twice a week, every day, every morning, every year, on Mondays, at noon, in the evening, etc.

1 Write the verbs in the correct columns. Listen and check. Listen and repeat.

close	play	march	need	carry	watch
wash	go	work	help	skate	take

/s/	/z/	/ɪz/
/f/, /k/, /p/, /t/	/s/, /ʃ/, /ʧ/, /ʤ/, /z/	after other sounds
		closes

2 Fill in the correct form of the verbs. Then match the sentences to the pictures.

play   ~~love~~   go   wear   drink   help

1 E Mike ..loves.. basketball.
2 ☐ My brother and I .... to school at 8 o'clock.
3 ☐ Carlos .... the guitar very well.
4 ☐ We .... our mum with the cooking.
5 ☐ I .... milk for breakfast.
6 ☐ My mum .... a uniform at work.

3 Complete the sentences.

— Long Form —

1 She ...does not... speak Italian.
2 They .... go to school.
3 We .... swim very well.
4 He .... watch TV every day.
5 You .... live in England.

— Short Form —

She ....doesn't.... speak Italian.
They .... go to school.
We .... swim very well.
He .... watch TV every day.
You .... live in England.

4 Write *doesn't* or *don't*.

1 Mr Jones *doesn't* teach Maths. He teaches Art.
2 The children .... get up late. They get up early.
3 I .... read comics. I read books.
4 It .... snow in summer. It snows in winter.
5 My brother .... like fish. He likes chicken.
6 You .... drink milk. You drink orange juice.

Interrogative	Questions	Short answers
Do I work? Do you work? Does he work? Does she work? Does it work? Do we work? Do you work? Do they work?	**Do I/we/you/they** work? **Does he/she/it** work?	Yes, I/we/they do. No, I/we/they don't. Yes, he/she/it does. No, he/she/it doesn't.

5 Write the questions and answers.

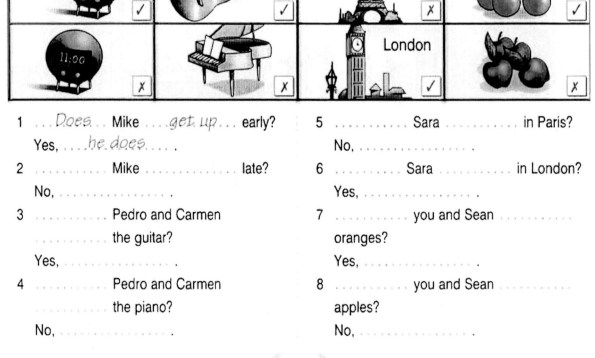

Mike	Pedro and Carmen	Sara	You and Sean
07:00 ✓	guitar ✓	Paris ✗	oranges ✓
11:00 ✗	piano ✗	London ✓	apples ✗

1 ...*Does*... Mike ...*get up*... early?
Yes, ...*he does*....
2 .... Mike .... late?
No, ...
3 .... Pedro and Carmen .... the guitar?
Yes, ...
4 .... Pedro and Carmen .... the piano?
No, ...
5 .... Sara .... in Paris?
No, ...
6 .... Sara .... in London?
Yes, ...
7 .... you and Sean .... oranges?
Yes, ...
8 .... you and Sean .... apples?
No, ...

6 Write the questions and answer them about you.

1 you / like chocolate
Do you like chocolate ?

4 your friends / listen to pop music
?

2 your best friend / like football
?

5 you / watch TV every day
?

3 you / live in a big house
?

6 your friends / play computer games
?

 Listen and repeat. Then act out.

Mum: When you go for dinner at Sam's house, use a knife and a fork.

Boy: Is it necessary, Mum?

Mum: Yes. We always use a knife and a fork when we eat.

Boy: But Mum, the soup never stays on a knife and a fork.

Adverbs of frequency

Adverbs of frequency tell us *how often* something happens.

She	always usually often sometimes rarely/seldom never	comes early.	He is	always usually often sometimes rarely/seldom never	late.

Read the sentences and circle.

- We use adverbs of frequency before / after the main verb.
- We use adverbs of frequency before / after the verb 'to be'.

Present Simple

7 Read and circle the correct sentence.

1 **(A)** Mike always walks to school.
   B Mike walks always to school.

2 **A** Does usually Alice go swimming on Sundays?
   B Does Alice usually go swimming on Sundays?

3 **A** Emma plays often tennis on Fridays.
   B Emma often plays tennis on Fridays.

4 **A** Meera is always on time for work.
   B Meera always is on time for work.

5 **A** Paul never drives to work.
   B Paul drives never to work.

6 **A** We sometimes go to the theatre at the weekend.
   B We go sometimes to the theatre at the weekend.

8 Write the sentences.

1 John is late. **(never)**
   John is never late.

2 The children eat ice cream. **(sometimes)**

3 I go to the cinema. **(often)**

4 We have lunch at a restaurant. **(seldom)**

5 You are polite to your teachers. **(always)**

6 Katie helps her mum. **(often)**

7 The boys are funny. **(sometimes)**

8 Ivan and I do our homework. **(always)**

9 Dad washes his car. **(never)**

10 Cara is very kind. **(usually)**

Speaking Activity

Interview your friend.

How often do you ...
- help in the house?
- eat fruit and vegetables?
- play sports?
- read comics?
- watch TV?
- eat at fast food restaurants?

How often do you help in the house?

I seldom help in the house.

Listen and repeat. Then act out.

Where is Mr Tims?

Mr Tims is sleeping at the moment. He always sleeps in the afternoon.

ZZZ...

Present Continuous – Present Simple

Read and match.

1 We use Present Continuous for things that

2 We use Present Simple for things that

a happen again and again.

b are happening now.

 Complete the table.

usually	at present	in the afternoons	at noon	today
now	often	always	on Mondays	at the moment

Time Expressions	
Present Simple	**Present Continuous**
usually, ...	. . . .
. . . .	. . . .
. . . .	. . . .

10 **Complete the sentences. Use the time expressions from the box.**

now	on Fridays	always (x3)	at the moment	every night (x2)

1 We watch the 9 o'clock news . . . . every night . . . . .

2 I . . . . have some toast and jam for breakfast.

3 My father is listening to music . . . .

4 At school we have our history lesson . . . .

5 I read a book or a magazine in bed . . . .

6 My grandfather . . . . sends me a birthday present.

7 My brother is doing his homework . . . .

8 My father . . . . buys a newspaper from the shop near his office.

11 Put the verbs into the *present simple* or the *present continuous*.

Emma 1) ....*is*.... (**be**) usually very busy on Saturdays. She 2) .... (**be**) in the school's swimming team. She usually 3) .... (**get up**) at eight o'clock, 4) .... (**have**) breakfast and 5) .... (**go**) swimming. This Saturday is a special Saturday for Emma. It 6) .... (**be**) her birthday. Can you see Emma? She 7) .... (**not/swim**). She 8) .... (**help**) her mother.

They 9) .... (**make**) Emma's birthday cake. Emma 10) .... (**love**) birthday cakes.

12 Read again and tick (✓) the best title for the story.

Emma's Special Saturday. ☐   Emma's Family. ☐   Emma's Daily Life. ☐

13 Put the verbs into the *present simple* or the *present continuous*.

1 Listen! The birds ...*are singing*... (**sing**) in the garden!

2 I often .... (**buy**) fruit from the greengrocer's.

3 My mother .... (**drink**) tea now.

4 Look at Tom and Jim! They .... (**walk**) up the hill.

5 That man .... (**laugh**) at the moment.

6 The cat .... (**play**) with a ball now.

7 We always .... (**wear**) warm clothes in winter.

8 He often .... (**eat**) a sandwich at lunchtime.

9 Be quiet! The girls .... (**sleep**).

10 How often .... (**you/go**) to the cinema?

11 They .... (**never/eat**) carrots.

12 They .... (**not/like**) potatoes.

13 What .... (**you/do**) now?

14 Can you see him? He .... (**walk**) down the street.

14 Look at the pictures and complete the poem.

talk   sing   do   read   tell   wash

My sister always 1) ....*talks*.... a lot,
She's always on the phone.
My brother never 2) .... up –
I sometimes 3) .... it on my own!

My father often 4) .... good jokes,
My mum usually 5) .... us stories.
We often 6) .... songs at night –
My family's never boring!

Writing Activity

Write about your family.

My sister always . . . .
She . . . .
My brother never . . . .
I sometimes . . . .

My father often . . . .
My mum usually . . . .
We often . . . .
My family's never boring!

1 Choose the correct item.

1 She _____ meat every day.
  A is eating   B eat   C eats

2 The baby _____ at the moment.
  A is sleeping   B sleeps   C sleep

3 I _____ to bed every night at 10:00 pm.
  A am going   B goes   C go

4 Dad _____ TV now.
  A is watching   B watches C watch

5 Mother always _____ the dishes.
  A is washing   B washes   C wash

6 Jane _____ a book at the moment.
  A is reading   B reads   C read

7 She _____ very quickly. Look!
  A is running   B runs   C run

8 I _____ my homework every day.
  A am doing   B do   C does

2 Rewrite the sentences.

1 I am late. (**always**)
  I'm always late.

2 She goes to the theatre on Fridays. (**usually**)
  ....

3 Does he visit his grandparents?
  (**sometimes**)
  ....

4 They come to our parties. (**often**)
  ....

5 My dad cooks dinner. (**never**)
  ....

6 My sister makes her bed. (**seldom**)
  ....

7 Do you watch TV in the afternoon?
  (**usually**)
  ....

8 We are rude to people. (**never**)
  ....

3 Put the verbs into the *present simple* or the *present continuous*.

It 1) *is* (be) Friday evening and my friends and I 2) .... (be) at the disco. Some people 3) .... (dance) on the dance floor. Some people 4) .... (sit) and 5) .... (drink) cola. My friends 6) .... (talk) and 7) .... (laugh) together. We 8) .... (go) to the disco every week. We usually 9) .... (drink) cola and 10) .... (dance).

Listening

4 |24| Look at the picture. Listen and draw lines. There is one example.

Sally

Peter

Sam

David

Jenny

Tom & Lee

5 |25| Song

We are playing in the sand
We're at the beach today
We always have fun at the beach
Hooray, hooray, hooray

We are eating sandwiches
We're eating ice creams, too
We love ice creams at the beach
You can have one, too!

We are swimming in the sea
We're having lots of fun
We're so glad that summer's here
We love the sea and sun

7

The Imperative

🎧 26 **Listen and repeat.**

We use the Imperative when we tell someone to do or not to do something.

Stand up.   Don't sit down.

---

1 **Circle the imperatives.**

Ahmed: Youssef, (help)! Come here.

Youssef: What's wrong, Ahmed?

Ahmed: Jump on the table. I can't reach the biscuits!

Youssef: OK. Now what?

Ahmed: Throw them down to me! Don't break the bowl.

Youssef: OK. Catch!

Ahmed: Ouch! Be careful, Youssef!

Simon says . . .

Follow your teacher's command only if it starts with *Simon says*.

Teacher: Simon says, clap your hands.

Students: (they clap their hands)

Teacher: Stamp your feet.

Students: (they remain as they were)

2 These are the Williams. What do you think their mother is saying? Use the verbs in the list.

jump	draw on the wall	come down	throw food
stop fighting	cry	go to bed	wash your face

1 *Don't jump!* ....
2 ....
3 ....
4 ....

5 ....
6 ....
7 ....
8 ....

Writing Activity

What does your mum tell you to do/not to do? Make a list with five everyday commands.

This is what my mum usually tells me:

– ....
– ....
– ....
– ....
– ....

Prepositions of Place

8

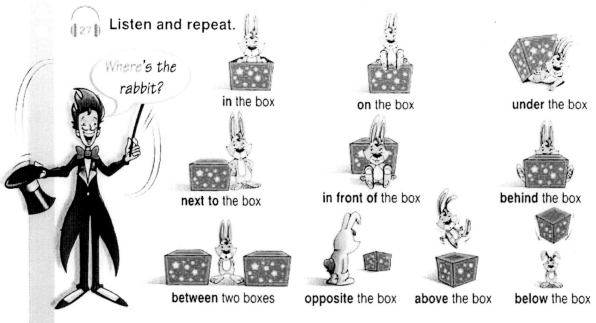

Listen and repeat.

Where's the rabbit?

in the box

on the box

under the box

next to the box

in front of the box

behind the box

between two boxes

opposite the box

above the box

below the box

We use prepositions of place to say where people, animals or things are.

---

1 Look at the picture and circle the correct preposition.

Peter is sitting 1) **between** / **opposite** his mother and father. They are watching TV. Peter's dog, Blackie, is sleeping 2) **behind** / **next to** the sofa. There is a coffee table 3) **behind** / **in front of** them. There is some tea and cakes 4) **on** / **in** it. Can you see Milly, Peter's cat? She's 5) **above** / **under** the coffee table. She's sleeping, too.

---

2 Read and write the names.

Tina is next to Paul.
Khalid is behind Rose.
Rose is next to Elisha.
Carlos is in front of Tina.
Paul is behind Elisha.

Tina

1   2   3

4   5   6

3 Look at the picture. Fill in: *on (x4)*, *above*, *under*, *behind*, *next to*.

This is Tom's room. Can you see him? He's 1) ...*on*... a rug 2) .... the bed. Tom's mother is very angry with him. His clothes are 3) .... the bed. There are empty cans of cola 4) .... the table, too. His toys are 5) .... the floor, 6) .... the chair, everywhere! Where are his books? They are 7) .... his bed. Look at the picture 8) .... his bed. It's so dirty! Oh Tom! Clean your room!

Picture Dictation

Your friend describes his room for you to draw it. Show the picture to your friend. Is your picture correct?

There is a bed in my room.

Writing Activity

Write about your friend's room.

My Friend's Room

by ....

This is my friend's room. There is ....

....

....

....

1 Match the sentences to the pictures.

Don't shout!   Don't touch the wall!   Don't eat those cakes!
Go to bed!   ~~Take your boots off, please!~~   Be careful!

1 *Take your boots off, please!*

2 ....

3 ....

4 ....

5 ....

6 ....

2 Complete the text with the words in the list.

under   between   behind   on (x2)   ~~in~~

The cat is sleeping 1) ......*in*...... its basket 2) .... the table. Dinner is 3) .... the table. Peter is sitting 4) .... Sally and Grandpa. John is 5) .... a chair. Grandma is bringing some food 6) .... a tray.

Listening

3 28 Look at the picture. Listen and colour and draw. There is one example.

4 29 Song

Stand up, sit down, keep moving
Stand up, sit down, keep moving
Stand up, sit down, keep moving
We're in the classroom today!

Stand up, sit down, keep moving,
stand up sit down, stand on one leg
And nod your head, keep moving
We're in the classroom today!

Stand up, sit down, keep moving,
stand up sit down, stand on one leg
And nod your head, turn around
Touch the ground, keep moving
We're in the classroom today!

Stand up, sit down, keep moving,
stand up sit down, stand on one leg
And nod your head, turn around
Touch the ground, wave your hands
Stamp your feet, keep moving
We're in the classroom today!

Stand up, sit down, keep moving,
stand up sit down, stand on one leg
And nod your head, turn around
Touch the ground, wave your hands
Stamp your feet, stand up, sit down
Relax now!
We're in the classroom today!

Prepositions of Time

30 Listen and repeat. Then act out.

We use prepositions of time to say *when* something happens.

in	at	on
in the morning	at 8 o'clock	on Sunday
in the afternoon	at noon	on Monday
in the evening	at night / midnight	on Tuesday
in November (months)	at the weekend	on Wednesday, etc.
in (the) summer (seasons)		on October 4th (dates)
in 2004 (years)		on Sunday afternoon

1 Choose the correct item.

1 In / **On** Saturday
2 In / At July
3 In / On 1984.
4 At / On March 25th
5 In / On Friday
6 In / At summer
7 In / On the morning
8 In / At 9 o'clock

9 In / On September 18th
10 In / At 1991
11 In / On August 4th
12 At / On Thursday afternoon
13 In / On the evening
14 On / In autumn
15 At / In the weekend

16 In / At midnight
17 At / On 2 o'clock
18 In / On winter
19 In / At noon
20 At / On Wednesday evening

2 Write *in*, *on* or *at*.

1 ...*In*... December
2 .... midnight
3 .... April
4 .... April 2nd

5 .... a quarter past six
6 .... noon
7 1998
8 .... spring

9 .... night
10 .... February 8th
11 .... Saturday night
12 .... Monday

3 Complete. Then tick (✓) the correct answer.

1 April Fool's Day is
   a) ....*on*.... April 1st. ✓
   b) .... autumn. ☐
   c) .... August. ☐

2 May Day is
   a) .... May. ☐
   b) .... summer. ☐
   c) .... May 31st. ☐

3 Mother's Day is
   a) .... winter. ☐
   b) .... a Sunday. ☐
   c) .... October. ☐

4 Independence Day is
   a) .... July 4th. ☐
   b) .... spring. ☐
   c) .... February. ☐

Speaking Activity

Ask and answer with your friend.

go to school	wake up	watch TV
meet your friends	go to bed	have breakfast
open presents	go on holiday	visit your grandparents
have dinner	play in the snow	do your homework
have English lessons	go to the park	

Student 1: When do you go to school?
Student 2: I go to school at nine o'clock. When do you meet your friends?

 Listen and repeat.

before / after

I get dressed **before** I have breakfast.

or

I have breakfast **after** I get dressed.

Prepositions of Time

4 Rewrite the sentences as in the example:

1 Tina drinks a glass of milk. She goes to bed.

Tina drinks a glass of milk
before she goes to bed.
Tina goes to bed after she
drinks a glass of milk.

2 Roy has lunch. He washes the dishes.

....
....

3 Alice has a shower. She gets dressed.

....

4 I watch TV. I go to bed.

....
....

5 My mother cooks lunch. She goes to work.

....
....

5 Fill in the gaps as in the example:

Scott's favourite day is Saturday. He usually gets up 1) . . . *at* . . . nine o'clock 2) . . . . the morning. He has breakfast and goes jogging. After that, he usually plays soccer with his friends. 3) . . . . noon, he has lunch with his parents. 4) . . . . the afternoon, he usually listens to music and 5) . . . . the evening, he sometimes goes to the cinema. Scott goes to bed late 6) . . . . night 7) . . . . Saturdays and he never gets up early 8) . . . . Sunday morning!

Writing Activity

Which is your favourite day? What do you do? Write.

My favourite day is . . . . I usually get up . . . .
. . . .
. . . .
. . . .
. . . .
. . . .

32 Listen and repeat. Then act out.

How much wool do you need to make a sweater?

A lot!

How many sheep do you need to make a sweater?

None. Sheep can't knit!

Read and complete the rules.

We use:
- How ....? with plural countable nouns.
- How ....? with uncountable nouns.

1 **33** Write the words in the correct column. Listen and check.

bread lemon water milk cheese pasta

meat coffee potato burger soup

apple olive oil strawberry banana yoghurt

Uncountable nouns	Countable nouns
bread,	lemon,

2 Read and circle the correct phrases.

1 How much / How many trees can you see?

2 How much / How many money have you got?

3 How much / How many eggs are there in the fridge?

4 How much / How many biscuits do you want?

5 How much / How many bread have we got?

6 How much / How many milk is there in the carton?

7 How much / How many boys are there in your class?

8 How much / How many glasses are there on the table?

9 How much / How many butter is there?

10 How much / How many books has he got?

3 Complete the questions and write the answers.

1	*How much*	milk is there?	*3 cartons*
2	*How many*	oranges are there?	*3 oranges*
3		bread is there?	
4		meat is there?	
5		bananas are there?	
6		coffee is there?	
7		tomatoes are there?	
8		biscuits are there?	
9		sugar is there?	
10		potatoes are there?	

64

We answer the questions in the following way:

	+	–
How many biscuits are there?	A lot!	Not many!
How much bread is there?	A lot!	Not much!

4 **Complete the dialogue with** *How much, How many, A lot, much* **or** *many*.

Kelly: Tina, let's ask Donna to join us for dinner tonight.

Tina: Have we got enough food? 1) …*How much*… meat is there in the fridge?

Kelly: Not 2) .... but there are three burgers.

Tina: OK. 3) .... potatoes have we got?

Kelly: 4) ....! About 5 kilos.

Tina: Great. We can make some chips to go with the burgers. 5) .... apples are there in the fridge? I want to make an apple pie.

Kelly: Not 6) .... We need to buy some. I can go to the supermarket.

Tina: OK. Let's call Donna then.

How much or How many?

Get into two groups. The teacher says a noun and the groups take it in turns to add *how much* or *how many*.

Teacher: cheese
Group A S1:   How much cheese? etc.

Writing Activity

You want to make an apple pie but you don't know how. Write a note to your mum and ask her to help you.

Mum,

I want to make an apple pie. Can you help me?

How ....

....

- flour?   - sugar?   Thanks,
- apples?   - butter?   ....

1 Choose the correct item.

1 It sometimes snows .... winter.
  (A) in   **B** at   **C** on

2 I have an English lesson .... Monday morning.
  A in   **B** at   **C** on

3 The boys eat lunch .... noon.
  A in   **B** at   **C** on

4 My favourite programme is .... half past seven.
  A in   **B** at   **C** on

5 I often watch TV .... the evening.
  A in   **B** at   **C** on

6 We go to bed .... 8 o'clock.
  A in   **B** at   **C** on

7 Ben's birthday is .... April 4th.
  A in   **B** at   **C** on

8 We usually go to the beach .... summer.
  A in   **B** at   **C** on

2 Look at the pictures and write questions and answers.

1  2  3  4

5  6  7  8

1 ...*How many tomatoes*... do we need?   ...*Not many.*...
2 .... is there in the fridge?   ....
3 .... is in the bottle?   ....
4 .... have we got?   ....
5 .... are there?   ....
6 .... do we need?   ....
7 .... have we got?   ....
8 .... are there?   ....

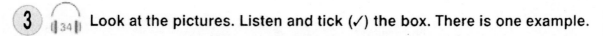

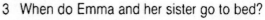 **3** ⏸34 **Look at the pictures. Listen and tick (✓) the box. There is one example.**

1 When does Billy have a guitar lesson?

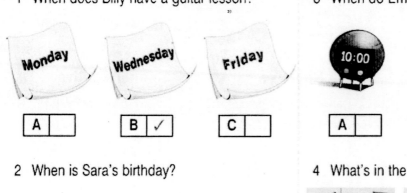

Monday   Wednesday   Friday

| A | | B | ✓ | C | |

3 When do Emma and her sister go to bed?

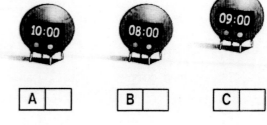

10:00   08:00   09:00

| A | | B | | C | |

2 When is Sara's birthday?

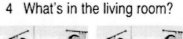

5ᵗʰ May   15ᵗʰ May   5ᵗʰ June

| A | | B | | C | |

4 What's in the living room?

| A | | B | | C | |

4 ⏸35

How much chicken have we got?
How much chocolate have we got?
How much cola have we got?
Can we have a picnic?

We've got chicken and chocolate, too
We've got cola for me and you
We've got biscuits and apples, too
We can have a picnic!

How many oranges have we got?
How many biscuits have we got?
How many apples have we got?
Can we have a picnic?

'Be going to'

Listen
and repeat.
Then act out.

I'm going to buy a small Japanese radio.

But how are you going to understand what they are saying?

Affirmative		Negative		Interrogative		
I	am/'m going to	I	am not/'m not going to	Am	I	going to?
You	are/'re going to	You	are not/aren't going to	Are	you	going to?
He		He		he		
She	is/'s going to	She	is not/isn't going to	Is	she	going to?
It		It			it	
We		We			we	
You	are/'re going to	You	are not/aren't going to	Are	you	going to?
They		They			they	

Short answers

Yes, I am. / No, I'm not.
Yes, you are. / No, you aren't.
Yes, he/she/it is. / No, he/she/it isn't.
Yes, we/you/they are. / No, we/you/they aren't.

We use be going to:
- **to talk about plans and intentions.**
  We **are going to travel** to France **next** summer.
- **when there is evidence that something is going to happen in the future.**
  Look at the grey clouds. It **is going to rain tonight**.

1 **Put the words in the correct order to make sentences as in the example:**

1 play / isn't / John / tennis / to / going
   John isn't going to play tennis....

2 tonight / we / to / watch / going / are / TV
   . . . .

3 Emily / is / read / going / that / to?
   . . . .

4 going / I / visit / am / to / my / next / grandma / weekend.
   . . . .

5 to / he / cook / isn't / dinner / going
   . . . .

2 Read and put a tick (✓) or a cross (✗).

1 The man is going to fall. ✓
2 The girls are going to play basketball. ☐
3 The woman is going to buy a cake. ☐
4 It's going to rain. ☐
5 The boys are going to play tennis. ☐
6 The cat is going to climb the tree. ☐

3 Write sentences.

1 (play/tennis)
I am going to play tennis.

2 (play/football)
They ....

3 (sleep)
We ....

4 (wash/the dishes)
She ....

5 (post/a letter)
He ....

6 (do/homework)
He ....

4 Alex is from London. He's going to spend a week in New York. Use the phrases below and the verbs in brackets to ask him some questions.

the Statue of Liberty	to Manhattan	a Broadway show
a street map	some autographs	in a five-star hotel

1 *Are you going to visit the Statue of Liberty* ? **(visit)**
2 ....? **(stay)**
3 ....? **(go)**
4 ....? **(buy)**
5 ....? **(see)**
6 ....? **(get)**

5 Write questions and answers.

	teacher	doctor	singer	football player
Fred		✓		
Rod & Ben			✓	
Joan	✓			
Ted				✓

1 Fred / singer? *Is Fred going to be a singer?*
No, he isn't. He's going to be a doctor.

2 Rod and Ben / teachers? ....
....

3 Joan / doctor? ....
....

4 Ted / singer? ....
....

6 Look at Julie's diary and write what her plans are for next week.

Monday: *meet Jane*	1 *Julie is going to meet Jane on Monday.*
Tuesday: *stay at home*	2 ....
Wednesday: *clean the house*	3 ....
Thursday: *buy new shoes*	4 ....
Friday: *visit my grandma*	5 ....
Saturday: *go to the theatre*	6 ....
Sunday: *have dinner with some friends*	7 ....

What's my lie?

Think of and say two things you are going to do next week and one you are not going to do. Ask your friend to guess which is the lie.

Student 1: I'm going to visit a museum. I'm going to sing in a concert. I'm going to play tennis.

Student 2: You aren't going to sing in a concert!

Student 1: That's right. Your turn now.

Writing Activity

What are your plans for next week? Write sentences.

1 I am going to	Monday:
2	Tuesday:
3	Wednesday:
4	Thursday:
5	Friday:
6	Saturday:
7	Sunday:

Like / Love / Hate + -ing form
Want + to form

37 **Listen and repeat. Then act out.**

Dad, do you like eating baked apples?

Yes. Why?

Our apple tree is on fire.

I hate eating cheese with holes in it.

Well, just eat the cheese and leave th holes on your plate

We often use the *-ing* form after the verbs like, love **and** hate.

I **like playing** tennis.   I **love eating** cakes.   I **hate playing** football.

---

1 **Put the verbs in brackets into the *-ing* form.**

Sally and her family love 1) . . . *going* . . . **(go)** to the park in the summer. They like 2) . . . . **(have)** picnics and love 3) . . . . **(sit)** on the grass. Sally's mum hates 4) . . . . **(make)** sandwiches so her dad always makes them. Sally and her brother love 5) . . . . **(play)** with a ball in the park. Sally's mum likes 6) . . . . **(lie)** on the blanket and loves

7) . . . . **(read)** her favourite magazines. Sally loves 8) . . . . **(listen)** to the birds singing in the trees and her brother likes 9) . . . . **(watch)** the people in the park. Sally's family likes the park because they love 10) . . . . **(be)** outdoors.

2 **Write the sentences.**

1 Ben / hate / play / tennis
.*Ben hates playing tennis.* . . . .

2 We / like / eat / chicken
. . . .

3 My friends / love / watch / TV
. . . .

4 Jenny / not like / read / comics
. . . .

5 I / hate / clean / my room
. . . .

6 The boys / love / listen / to music
. . . .

7 You / not like / wear / hats
. . . .

8 My dad / like / drive / his car
. . . .

3 Write questions and answers.

1 the girls / eat chocolate

(like) *Do the girls like eating chocolate?*

(Yes, love) *Yes, they love eating chocolate.*

2 Tom / do his homework

(like) ....

(No, not like) ....

3 the horse / jump

(like) ....

(No, hate) ....

4 Sam / get up early

(like) ....

(No, hate) ....

5 the children / go to the circus

(like) ....

(Yes, like) ....

6 the baby / take medicine

(like) ....

(No, hate) ....

7 Dad / wash the car

(like) ....

(No, not like) ....

8 they / drink cola

(like) ....

(Yes, like) ....

38 Listen and repeat. Then act out.

We use the to form after the verb want: I want to buy a new computer.

4 Look at the pictures and write sentences. Use the words from the box.

doctors   singer   pilot   dentist   clown   footballer

1 Roy ...wants to be a singer.........

2 Sue and Beth ....

2 Carlos ....

4 Adam ....

5 Katie ....

6 Kurt ....

5 Fill in the correct form of the verbs.

Tina: I want 1) *to go* (go) somewhere this weekend. I don't want 2) .... (stay) inside!

George: I want 3) .... (visit) my cousin in London. Do you want 4) .... (come) with me?

Tina: Great! When do you want 5) .... (leave)?

George: I want 6) .... (start) early in the morning. I don't want 7) .... (travel) when there is a lot of traffic.

Tina: OK. We can meet at seven at my house.

George: Great. See you then.

Speaking Activity

Complete the questions. Then ask your friend and write his/her answers.

1 Do you like ... *playing* ... (play) computer games? ....
2 Do you like .... (listen) to music? ....
3 Do you like .... (watch) cartoons? ....
4 Do you like .... (go) fishing? ....
5 Do you like .... (skate)? ....
6 Do you like .... (swim)? ....

Writing Activity

Write what your friend likes/doesn't like doing.

My friend ....

....

....

....

....

....

1 Write the sentences. Use *be going to* and the *present continuous*.

 (eat)

They are going to eat.

They are eating.

 (have/a bath)

. . . .

. . . .

. . . .

. . . .

 (wash/his car)

. . . .

. . . .

. . . .

. . . .

. . . .

. . . .

2 Write sentences.

1 I / hate / eat / fish

I hate eating fish.

2 You / not like / play / the piano

. . . .

3 My mum / want / listen / to music

. . . .

4 We / like / drink / milk

. . . .

5 My friends / hate / wash / the dishes

. . . .

6 Katie / not like / ride / her bike

. . . .

7 I / want / read / my magazine

. . . .

8 The boys / love / watch / films

. . . .

Listening

3 🎧 39 **Look at the pictures. What is Sally going to do next week?**
Listen and draw lines. There is one example.

4 🎧 40 **Song** ✏️

I'm going to see my friends tomorrow	We're going to run and jump tomorrow
We're going to go to the park tomorrow	We're going to ride our bikes tomorrow
We're going to play outdoors tomorrow	We're going to play football tomorrow
We can play all day	We can play all day
We're going to play tomorrow	We're going to sail our boats tomorrow
Hip, Hip, Hooray, tomorrow	We're going to fly our kites tomorrow
We're going to play tomorrow	We're going to eat ice cream tomorrow
We can play all day	We can play all day

Listen and repeat. Then act out.

We use must to talk about obligation or necessity.
You **must** do your homework every day.

We use mustn't to talk about prohibition.
You **mustn't** eat in class.

1 What *must/mustn't* you do in a park? Look at the signs and write sentences.

1 (drive slowly)

You must drive
slowly.

2 (walk on the paths)

3 (swim in the pond)

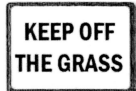

4 (keep off the grass)

5 (park here)

6 (throw rubbish on the street)

2 What does Billy's mum say? Write *must* or *mustn't*.

1 You *must* tidy your room.
2 You .... go to bed late.
3 You .... get up early.
4 You .... eat your dinner.
5 You .... be good.
6 You .... play loud music.

Speaking Activity

What *must/mustn't* you do in class? Talk with your friend. Think about:

eat in class	be late	play football in class	do homework
be polite	be rude	read comics in class	listen to the teacher

Student A: We mustn't eat in class.
Student B: Yes, of course. And we must be polite.

Writing Activity

Write rules for your class.

These are the rules for our class:

We ....

....

....

....

....

Listen and repeat. Then act out.

Affirmative	Negative		Interrogative
	Long form	**Short form**	
I have to go	I do not have to go	I don't have to go	Do I have to go?
You have to go	You do not have to go	You don't have to go	Do you have to go?
He has to go	He does not have to go	He doesn't have to go	Does he have to go?
She has to go	She does not have to go	She doesn't have to go	Does she have to go?
It has to go	It does not have to go	It doesn't have to go	Does it have to go?
We have to go	We do not have to go	We don't have to go	Do we have to go?
You have to go	You do not have to go	You don't have to go	Do you have to go?
They have to go	They do not have to go	They don't have to go	Do they have to go?

Short answers

Do you have to go?	Yes, I/we do. – No, I/we don't.
Does he/she/it have to go?	Yes, he/she/it does. – No, he/she/it doesn't.
Do they have to go?	Yes, they do. – No, they don't.

We use have to when we talk about things that are necessary to do. We *cannot choose* to do something else.
I **have to** wear a uniform at school. (I cannot choose to go to this school without a uniform. It's obligatory.)

We use don't have to when we talk about things that are not necessary to do.
You **don't have to** come to the party with me. (It's not necessary to come with me but you can come if you want to.)

3 Read and circle all the examples of *have to*. What does Mike have to do today?

Hi, my name is Mike. Today I (have to) do a lot of things. First, I have to clean my room. Then, I have to look after my little sister because my father has to go shopping. Then later, I have to help my father make a big chocolate cake for my mum's birthday party this evening. Today is a very busy day but a very nice one, too!

4 Complete the dialogue with *have to* in the correct form.

Sandra: Tim, I've got some information about Jimmy's new school.

Tim: Great! 1) *Does he have to wear* **(he/wear)** a uniform?

Sandra: Yes, he does. 2) .... **(we/buy)** him a new one.

Tim: OK. 3) .... **(I/drive)** him to school?

Sandra: No, 4) .... **(you/drive)** him there. He can take the school bus.

Tim: Excellent. 5) .... **(he/be)** at school early?

Sandra: Well, the school bus comes at 7:30 am. 6) .... **(he/be)** ready by then.

Tim: That's not bad. Let's talk to Jimmy then.

Speaking Activity

Complete the questions. Then ask your friend to answer the questions.

At home ...

1 ... *Do you have to* ... wash the dishes? **(you)**

....

2 .... cook all the meals? **(your mum)**

....

3 .... walk to school? **(you)**

....

4 .... help with the housework? **(your dad)**

....

5 .... clean his/her room? **(your brother/ sister)**

....

6 .... wash your own clothes? **(wash)**

....

Write five things that you have to do at home.

I have to . . . .

. . . .

. . . .

 Listen and repeat. Then act out.

> We use **Shall** ...? when we want to do something for a person.
> **Shall** I make you a cup of tea?

5 Complete the dialogues with the questions.

- Shall I get a DVD?
- Shall I open it?
- Shall I call a taxi?
- Shall I make some sandwiches?

1 A: Look at the time! It's time to go.
   B: *Shall I call a taxi?*
   A: Yes, please.

2 A: I'm starving.
   B: . . . .
   A: That's lovely, thank you.

3 A: There is someone at the door.
   B: . . . .
   A: Yes, please!

4 A: There's nothing on TV tonight.
   B: . . . .
   A: That sounds great!

Listen and repeat.

My manners at the table
Are always very good.
When I want to eat, I say:
Please, may I have some food?
May I have some cola?
May I have dessert?
May I leave the table, now?
Because my tummy hurts!

Read the poem again. Why does the boy's tummy hurt?

We use may to ask for permission.
A: **May I** open the door?
B: **Yes**, you may. / **No**, you may not.

6 Imagine that you are a guest in a friend's house. Ask politely for what you want using *may*.

1 You want to open the window because it's very hot.

May I open the window, please?
....

2 You want to watch TV.
....

3 You want to have a sandwich.
....

4 You want to have some orange juice.
....

5 You want to call your mother.
....

Where am I?

You are in two groups. The teacher says a sentence and you try to guess the place. Each correct answer wins a point. The team with the most points wins.

Teacher: You must be quiet. Everyone is reading!
Group 1 Student 1: You are at a library!
Teacher: Correct. 1 point for Group 1.

Past Simple (Was – Were)

 Listen and repeat. Then act out.

Affirmative	Negative	
	Long form	Short form
I was	I was not	I wasn't
You were	You were not	You weren't
He was	He was not	He wasn't
She was	She was not	She wasn't
It was	It was not	It wasn't
We were	We were not	We weren't
You were	You were not	You weren't
They were	They were not	They weren't

Time expressions with the past simple

yesterday	last year	two days ago	yesterday afternoon
last week	two weeks ago	then	last night
last month	two months ago	yesterday morning	two hours ago

We use the past simple for actions which happened at a definite time in the past.
I **was** at the circus **yesterday**. (When was I at the circus? Yesterday.)

 Choose the correct item.

1 I **was** / were at my friend's house yesterday.

2 The girls **was** / **were** happy last week.

3 Grandma **was** / **were** at the supermarket two hours ago.

4 You **was** / **were** late for school yesterday.

5 Sam **was** / **were** tired last night.

6 Marek and Anna **was** / **were** bored last Saturday.

7 The dog **was** / **were** in the garden yesterday.

8 You and Ahmed **was** / **were** at school last Monday.

9 It **was** / **were** sunny last week.

10 We **was** / **were** at the cinema last night.

2 Write the sentences in the *past simple*.

TODAY

1 They are at the cinema.
2 I'm not happy.
3 The film is scary.
4 Is he in London?
5 What is for lunch?
6 George isn't very friendly.
7 Are they happy?
8 It's very hot!

YESTERDAY

They were at the cinema.

....
....
....
....
....
....
....

Interrogative	Short answers
Was I ...?	Yes, I was. / No, I wasn't.
Were you ...?	Yes, you were. / No, you weren't.
Was he ...?	Yes, he was. / No, he wasn't.
Was she ...?	Yes, she was. / No, she wasn't.
Was it ...?	Yes, it was. / No, it wasn't.
Were we ...?	Yes, we were. / No, we weren't.
Were you ...?	Yes, you were. / No, you weren't.
Were they ...?	Yes, they were. / No, they weren't.

3 Tina was in London last Sunday. Write questions and answers.

1 (London/beautiful)
Was London
beautiful?
Yes, it was.

2 (the people/kind)
....
Yes, ...

3 (the weather/good)
....
No, ...

4 (the hotel/nice)
....
No, ...

5 (your room/small)
....
Yes, ...

6 (the museums/interesting)
....
Yes, ...

Past Simple (Was – Were)

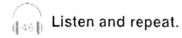

🎧 46 Listen and repeat.

There was / There were

Fifty years ago, there was a park opposite our house. There were a lot of children there every day.

4 Spot the differences. Complete the sentences with *was*, *were* and a number.

1 Yesterday there ...*were two*... children in the park.   Today there are three.

2 Yesterday there .... bird in the sky.   Today there are four.

3 Yesterday there .... butterflies.   Today there is one.

4 Yesterday there .... dog.   Today there are two.

5 Yesterday there .... boats on the lake.   Today there are three.

6 Yesterday there .... frogs.   Today there is one.

5 Write *was* or *were*.

1 It ...*was*... hot last summer.
2 There .... two cakes in the fridge yesterday.
3 The boys .... at the library last Wednesday.
4 Mum .... at work yesterday.

5 There .... a cat at the window an hour ago.
6 My friends .... at school yesterday.
7 James .... at my party last night.
8 There .... a lot of people at the park yesterday.

Speaking Activity

What were you and your friend like when you were children? Answer the questions. Then interview your friend.

	Me	My friend
1 Were you noisy or quiet?	....	....
2 Were you polite or rude?	....	....
3 What was your favourite colour?	....	....
4 What was your favourite food?	....	....
5 Who was your favourite cartoon character?	....	....
6 What was your favourite toy?	....	....

Writing Activity

What were you like when you were a child? Write. Use your answers from the Speaking Activity.

When I was a child I ....
....
....
....
....

1 Choose the correct item.

1 You **must** / **mustn't** brush your teeth after meals. It's good for your teeth.
2 **Shall** / **Have** I make you a cup of coffee?
3 You **have to** / **don't have to** wear a uniform at our school. You can wear anything you like.
4 You **must** / **mustn't** swim here. It's dangerous.
5 You **must** / **mustn't** have a bath. You are so dirty!
6 He **has to** / **doesn't have to** get up early tomorrow. His flight is at 6:30 in the morning!
7 **Have** / **Shall** I make you a sandwich?
8 **Have** / **May** I go out, Miss?

2 Write the questions and answers.

1 Sam / in London / last week?
Was Sam in London last week?
No, he wasn't. He was in Paris.

2 Jim and Tom / at school / yesterday?

3 the girls / at the zoo / yesterday?

4 you and your friend / at the cinema / last night?

3 🎧 47 Look at the pictures. Listen and draw lines. There is one example.

• Where was Kelly last week?

| Monday |
| Tuesday |
| Wednesday |
| Thursday |
| Friday |
| Saturday |
| Sunday |

4 🎧 48 Song 🎤

I was in my bed three hours ago
I was in my house two hours ago
I was on the bus one hour ago
Now I am at school!

I was at the beach four days ago
I was in the park three days ago
I was at the zoo two days ago
Now I am at school!

I was in the garden on Saturday
I was in my treehouse last Sunday
I was at my friend's house last Monday
Now I am at school!

Past Simple (Had – Could)

Listen and repeat. Then act out.

Did the film have a happy ending?

I think so. Everyone was happy when the film was over.

Had is the past simple of the verb 'have (got)'.

Affirmative	Negative	
	Long form	**Short form**
I had	I did not have	I didn't have
You had	You did not have	You didn't have
He had	He did not have	He didn't have
She had	She did not have	She didn't have
It had	It did not have	It didn't have
We had	We did not have	We didn't have
You had	You did not have	You didn't have
They had	They did not have	They didn't have

1 Complete the sentences. Write *had* or *didn't have*.

Yesterday ...

1 I ...had... pasta for lunch.

2 I .....didn't have..... a shower in the morning.

3 I .... breakfast. I was in a hurry.

4 I .... a lovely time at Julie's party.

5 I .... a long walk with Rita in the park.

6 I .... an English lesson.

7 I .... dinner with my friend Frank.

8 I .... a quiet day.

90

2 Look at the picture and write sentences.

When Jamie was a young boy ...

1 (long hair)   *He didn't have long hair. He had short hair.*

2 (dark hair) ....

3 (cat) ....

4 (roller-skates) ....

5 (toy bus) ....

Interrogative	Short answers
Did I have ...?	Yes, I did. / No, I didn't.
Did you have ...?	Yes, you did. / No, you didn't.
Did he have ...?	Yes, he did. / No, he didn't.
Did she have ...?	Yes, she did. / No, she didn't.
Did it have ...?	Yes, it did. / No, it didn't.
Did we have ...?	Yes, we did. / No, we didn't.
Did you have ...?	Yes, you did. / No, you didn't.
Did they have ...?	Yes, they did. / No, they didn't.

3 Look at the picture. Write questions and answers.

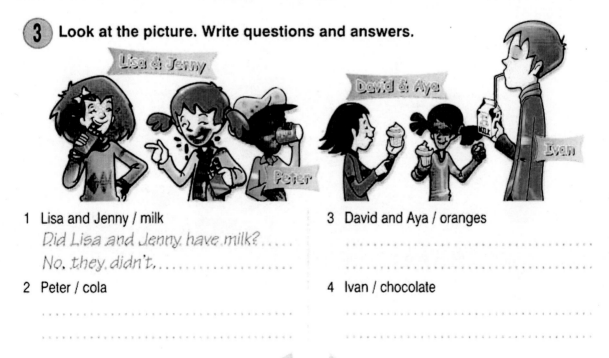

1 Lisa and Jenny / milk
Did Lisa and Jenny have milk?
No, they didn't.

2 Peter / cola
....
....

3 David and Aya / oranges
....
....

4 Ivan / chocolate
....
....

4 Complete the dialogue with the correct form of *have*.

Dad: Bob, what 1) *did you have* (you/have) for lunch? You 2) .... (not/have) any chocolate. Right?

Bob: Erm, no, I 3) ....

Dad: Are you sure?

Bob: Well, you know me, Dad. My memory is not very good!

Dad: What about you, Emma?

Emma: I only 4) .... (have) a sandwich, Dad. No chocolate!

Dad: 5) .... (you/have) some juice, too?

Emma: Yes, I 6) ....

Dad: There wasn't any juice in the fridge, Emma!

Emma: Really? My memory isn't very good, either!

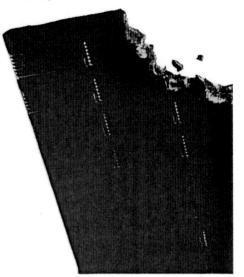

Brain GYM

GAME

Look at the table for two minutes. Close your books and play the game.

Student 1: What did you have for lunch?
Student 2: I had 3A.
Student 1: Did you have chicken?
Student 2: Yes, I did. Your turn now.

Could

🎧 50 **Listen and repeat.**

Amadeus Mozart *could* play the piano when he was four.

Albert Einstein *couldn't* spell.

> *Could* is the past simple of the verb 'can'.

Affirmative	Negative
I/You could swim	I/You could not (couldn't) swim
He/She/It could swim	He/She/It could not (couldn't) swim
We/You/They could swim	We/You/They could not (couldn't) swim

Interrogative	Short answers
Could I/you swim?	Yes, I/you could. – No, I/you couldn't.
Could he/she/it swim?	Yes, he/she/it could. – No, he/she/it couldn't.
Could we/you/they swim?	Yes, we/you/they could. – No, we/you/they couldn't.

5 **Look at the pictures. Complete the sentences with *could* or *couldn't*.**

- What could Amy do when she was nine?

1 She ...*could*... swim.
2 She .... climb.
3 She .... sing.
4 She .... read.
5 She .... ride a horse.
6 She .... play the piano.

Past Simple (Had – Could)

6 What happened yesterday? Match and write sentences.

1 Kelly / be tired
2 Harry / have a toothache
3 The supermarket / not be open
4 Isabel / be ill
5 Tom / be away
6 There / be a lot of rain

a she / not go to school
b he / not come to the birthday party
c she / not water the plants
d we / not go out and play
e he / not eat his food
f Jim / not go shopping

1 Kelly was tired, so she couldn't water the plants.
2
3
4
5
6

7 What could/couldn't you do when you were five? Put a tick (✓) or a cross (✗). Tell the class.

- swim ☐
- play computer games ☐
- speak English ☐
- run ☐
- count to 20 ☐
- sing ☐
- read and write ☐
- climb ☐
- ride a bike ☐
- dance ☐

When I was five I couldn't swim but I could play computer games.

Writing Activity

Write what you could/couldn't do when you were five.

When I was five I

Past Simple (Regular Verbs)

 Listen and repeat. Then act out.

A: Why did the bird cancel his trip?
B: Because the feather forecast wasn't good.

Affirmative	Negative	
	Long form	**Short form**
I walked	I did not walk	I didn't walk
You walked	You did not walk	You didn't walk
He walked	He did not walk	He didn't walk
She walked	She did not walk	She didn't walk
It walked	It did not walk	It didn't walk
We walked	We did not walk	We didn't walk
You walked	You did not walk	You didn't walk
They walked	They did not walk	They didn't walk

We use the past simple for actions that happened at a definite time in the past.
I **played** basketball **yesterday.**

How do we form the past simple? Choose.

A subject + verb -ed
B subject + was/were + verb -ed

Spelling

Look at the spelling of these verbs:

love – lov**ed**   stop – sto**pped**   travel – travel**led**

stud**y** – stud**ied**   BUT   play – play**ed**

95

Past Simple (Regular Verbs)

1 Write the *past simple* of the following verbs.

1	watch	*watched*	6	walk	11	cry
2	clean		7	shop	12	water
3	return		8	look	13	drop
4	stop		9	tidy	14	call
5	stay		10	smile	15	stay

2 **Write the verbs in the right column. Listen and check. Listen and repeat.**

visit	love	look	shout	walk	play
clean	talk	want	wash	try	paint

/t/	/d/	/id/
/k/, /s/, /ʃ/, /tʃ/, /dʒ/, /f/, /p/	after other sounds	/t/, /d/
		visited

3

1 I talked to Jane an hour **last** / <u>**ago**</u>.
2 We played tennis **last** / **ago** Sunday.
3 He phoned me two hours **last** / **ago**.
4 It rained **last** / **yesterday**.
5 They travelled by plane **last** / **ago** month.

6 I walked the dog five hours **ago** / **last**.
7 I listened to music **last** / **ago** night.
8 He worked in London **last** / **ago** year.
9 We played tennis **yesterday** / **ago**.
10 Tim cooked dinner **last** / **yesterday** Monday.

4 **Complete the text with the *past simple*.**

Yesterday my family and I 1) ....*visited*.... **(visit)** my grandparents. My mum 2) .... **(help)** my grandma with the housework. My dad 3) .... **(clean)** the windows. My brother and I 4) .... **(watch)** cartoons on TV. Later, we 5) .... **(play)** outside in the garden. We 6) .... **(climb)** up the tree to get to the treehouse. We 7) .... **(stay)** there all afternoon. Then our mum 8) .... **(call)** us because it was time to go. Our grandparents 9) .... **(kiss)** us goodbye and we 10) .... **(return)** home.

5 Complete the text with the *past simple*.

Yesterday my sister and I 1) *helped* (help) our mum in the house. First, we 2) .... (clean) our rooms and then we 3) .... (wash) our clothes. After that, we 4) .... (cook) some pasta. The pasta 5) .... (not/be) very good, Harris, but our mum 6) .... (be) happy to eat it. She 7) .... (not/want) to show that the food 8) .... (be) awful! Our Mum is so kind!

6 Mum usually does the housework but yesterday Dad did the housework. Write the sentences.

Usually		Yesterday
	1 clean / the house *Mum usually cleans the house. Yesterday, Dad cleaned the house.*	
	2 wash / the dishes	
	3 cook / dinner	
	4 iron / the clothes	
	5 walk / the dog	

Past Simple (Regular Verbs)

7 Write the sentences in the negative.

1 We studied in the library yesterday.
We didn't study in the library yesterday.

2 Pedro played football last Sunday.

3 I watched TV last night.

4 Aya listened to music yesterday evening.

5 The cat climbed a tree yesterday morning.

6 It rained last week.

7 He smiled at me.

8 George tidied his room an hour ago.

8 Write sentences.

	clean the house	water the flowers	watch TV	listen to the radio
Elena	✓	✓		
Youssef			✓	✓
Mr & Mrs Hill	✓		✓	
Carmen		✓	✓	

1 Elena *cleaned the house and watered the flowers yesterday.*
She didn't watch TV or listen to the radio.

2 Youssef

3 Mr and Mrs Hill

4 Carmen

Interrogative	Short answers
Did I walk ...?	Yes, I did. / No, I didn't.
Did you walk ...?	Yes, you did. / No, you didn't.
Did he walk ...?	Yes, he did. / No, he didn't.
Did she walk ...?	Yes, she did. / No, she didn't.
Did it walk ...?	Yes, it did. / No, it didn't.
Did we walk ...?	Yes, we did. / No, we didn't.
Did you walk ...?	Yes, you did. / No, you didn't.
Did they walk ...?	Yes, they did. / No, they didn't.

9 **Read and tick (✓).**

1 Did Susie play football last Saturday?
   Yes, she did. ☑
   Yes, he did. ☐

2 Did it snow last winter?
   No, it didn't. ☐
   No, they didn't. ☐

3 Did Mum and Dad finish work late last
   night?
   Yes, they did. ☐
   Yes, she did. ☐

4 Did Mark watch TV yesterday?
   Yes, he did. ☐
   Yes, she did. ☐

5 Did the children walk to school yesterday
   morning?
   Yes, they did. ☐
   Yes, we did. ☐

6 Did you visit your friend last week?
   Yes, I did. ☐
   Yes, she did. ☐

10 **Complete the questions and answers.**

1 ..... _Did_ ..... you cook breakfast yesterday morning? No, ... _I didn't_ ....
2 .... the boys watch a film last night? Yes, ...
3 .... Mum clean the house yesterday? No, ...
4 .... your grandparents visit you last weekend? Yes, ...
5 .... Steve play basketball last weekend? Yes, ...
6 .... you and Claire clean your rooms last Monday? No, ...

11 What did the Smiths do last Sunday? Write the questions and answers.

1 the girls / play tennis
   Did the girls play tennis?
   No, they didn't.

2 Mum / listen to music

3 Dad / cook burgers

4 the dogs / stay in the car

5 the boy / collect shells

6 it / rain

History Mix-up

GAME

Are you good at history? Correct the sentences. You've got two minutes!

1 King Henry VIII lived in Spain.
   King Henry VIII didn't live in
   Spain. He lived in England.

2 Rudolph Nureyev painted *Sunflowers*.

3 Charlie Chaplin composed music.

4 Vincent Van Gogh danced in big theatres.

5 Pablo Picasso lived in England.

6 Amadeus Mozart acted in films.

12 Complete the email.

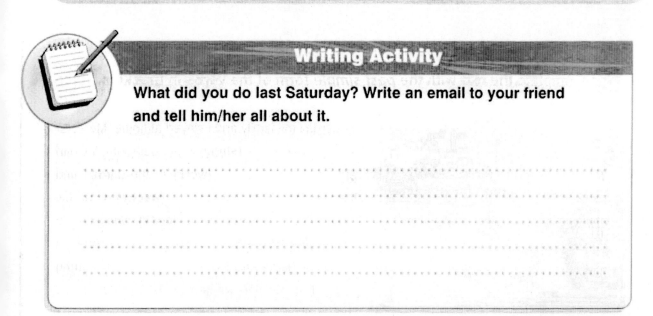

Dear Kim,

Here are some 1) *photos* from the museum we 2) *visited* **(visit)** last Friday. It was great!

We all 3) .... **(travel)** on the school 4) .... At the museum we 5) .... **(look)** at some paintings and some statues.

Then we 6) .... **(watch)** a film about the Tudors. On the way back we

7) .... **(stop)** at a park. We 8) .... **(play)** some games there and

listened to 9) ....

It was a fantastic day! I hope you like the photos.

Love,

Tracy

Writing Activity

What did you do last Saturday? Write an email to your friend and tell him/her all about it.

....
....
....
....
....

1 Look at the pictures and complete the sentences.

When Sally was twelve ...

1 She ...... *had* ...... a cat.

2 She ..... *could* ..... swim.

3 She .... a rabbit.

4 She .... run.

5 She .... ride a bike.

6 She .... a computer.

7 She .... a baby brother.

8 She .... dance.

2 Complete the text with the *past simple* form of the verbs in brackets.

Yesterday my family and I stayed at home. My sister 1) ...*studied*... **(study)** in her bedroom. My dad 2) .... **(work)** in the garden and then he 3) .... **(wash)** his car. My mum 4) .... **(cook)** dinner in the kitchen. My brother 5) .... **(play)** a computer game and I 6) .... **(tidy)** my bedroom. Later, we all 7) .... **(have)** dinner and then we 8) .... **(watch)** a film on TV.

Listening

3 🎧 53 **Listen and tick (✓) the box. There is one example.**

1 What did Ben have for breakfast?

A ☐   B ✓   C ☐

3 What did Ben have for lunch?

  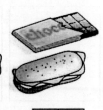

A ☐   B ☐   C ☐

2 What lesson did Ben have first?

A ☐   B ☐   C ☐

4 What did Ben watch on TV?

A ☐   B ☐   C ☐

4 🎧 54  Song

I had breakfast, I had breakfast yesterday
I played football, I played football yesterday
I had breakfast, I played football
My friends and I played football
We played a game of football yesterday

Oh, we all had lots and lots of fun
Yes, we all had lots and lots of fun
We had fun together, fun together
We had a great day in the sun

I had cola, I had cola yesterday
I had ice cream, I had ice cream yesterday
I had cola, I had ice cream
My friends and I had ice cream
We all had lots of ice cream yesterday

Past Simple (Irregular Verbs)

(55) Listen and repeat. Then act out.

I went fly-fishing with my dad yesterday.

I caught a blue bottle.

Did you catch anything?

Some verbs in the past simple do not take -ed. We call them irregular verbs.

I **played** basketball yesterday. (regular verb)

I **went** to the park yesterday. (irregular verb)

Affirmative	Negative	
	Long form	**Short form**
I went	I did not go	I didn't go
You went	You did not go	You didn't go
He went	He did not go	He didn't go
She went	She did not go	She didn't go
It went	It did not go	It didn't go
We went	We did not go	We didn't go
You went	You did not go	You didn't go
They went	They did not go	They didn't go

1 (56) **Look at the Irregular Verbs list on page 160 and complete the table. Listen and check. Listen and repeat.**

Present	Past		Present	Past
1 is / are	was / were	13 make		
2 break	broke	14 meet		
3 buy		15 put		
4 come		16 read		
5 cut		17		rode
6	cost	18		ran
7 drink		19 see		
8 drive		20 sit		
9	ate	21		swam
10 get		22 take		
11 have		23 tell		
12	went	24		wrote

104

2 Complete the sentences with a verb from the box in the *past simple*.

break	buy	have	drink	make	write

1 She ...*made*... a cake an hour ago.

2 She .... a hat last week.

3 Juan .... a letter yesterday.

4 They .... a lot of cola last night.

5 She .... her arm last week.

6 He .... a shower two minutes ago.

3 Write the sentences in the negative.

1 We went to the cinema yesterday.
We didn't go to the cinema yesterday.

2 John read a comic yesterday afternoon.
....

3 My friends came to my house last weekend.
....

4 You bought a new CD yesterday.
....

5 I swam in the sea last summer.
....

6 Emma told me a joke yesterday.
....

7 The cat ate a fish last night.
....

8 You and Jim made sandwiches for lunch yesterday.
....

9 Dad drove to work yesterday morning.
....

10 Our grandparents sent us an email last week.
....

4 Complete the text with the *past simple* form of the verbs in brackets.

Last Saturday my dad 1) ....*took*.......... (take) my friend, Harry, and me to the circus. My Dad 2) .... (buy) us some popcorn and orange juice. We 3) .... (see) lots of things at the circus. There 4) .... (be) some lions. They 5) .... (do) some tricks; they 6) .... (jump) through hoops. A girl 7) .... (ride) an elephant around the ring. We 8) .... (have) a lovely time at the circus.

5 Read the text in Ex. 4 again and find three mistakes in the picture.

1 *My Dad didn't buy us ice cream. He bought us some popcorn.* ....

2 ....

   ....

3 ....

   ....

6 Write what Marita did or didn't do yesterday.

1 go shopping ✗	1 *Marita didn't go shopping yesterday.*
2 clean the house ✓	2 ....
3 feed the cat ✓	3 ....
4 phone Mary ✗	4 ....
5 watch a film on TV ✗	5 ....
6 visit her grandparents ✓	6 ....
7 buy them a cake ✓	7 ....

Interrogative	Short answers
Did I go ...?	Yes, I did. / No, I didn't.
Did you go ...?	Yes, you did. / No, you didn't.
Did he go ...?	Yes, he did. / No, he didn't.
Did she go ...?	Yes, she did. / No, she didn't.
Did it go ...?	Yes, it did. / No, it didn't.
Did we go ...?	Yes, we did. / No, we didn't.
Did you go ...?	Yes, you did. / No, you didn't.
Did they go ...?	Yes, they did. / No, they didn't.

7 **Complete the questions about yesterday. Answer them about you.**

1 What time ...*did*... you *get up* ? **(get up)** .....*I got up at* ....

2 What .... you .... for breakfast? **(have)** ....

3 .... you .... a shower in the morning? **(have)** ....

4 What time .... you .... to school? **(go)** ....

5 .... you .... by bus? **(go)** ....

6 What .... you .... for lunch? **(eat)** ....

7 .... you .... a sandwich? **(eat)** ....

8 When .... you .... home from school? **(come)** ....

9 .... you .... your homework in the afternoon? **(do)** ....

10 What time .... you .... at night? **(go to sleep)** ....

8 **Complete the dialogue.**

Dustin: Hello, Fiona. How was your weekend?
     1) ...*Did you have*... **(you/have)** a good time?

Fiona: Yes, I 2) ...*did*... I 3) .... **(go)**
     to the zoo last Saturday.

Dustin: 4) .... **(you/see)** the monkeys?

Fiona: No, I 5) .... but I 6) ....
     (see) the baby penguins. They were great! I even
     7) .... **(feed)** them!

Dustin: 8) .... **(you/take)** any photos?

Fiona: Yes, I 9) .... Look!

Past Simple (Irregular Verbs)

We use the present continuous for actions happening now.

Look! He's playing football.

We use 'be going to' to talk about plans and intentions.

He is going to play football next Monday.

We use the present simple for habits and permanent actions.

He always plays football on Fridays.

We use the past simple to talk about actions that happened at a definite time in the past.

He played football last Friday.

9 Complete the sentences with one word or phrase from the box.

| usually | at the moment | every morning | next week |
| yesterday | last night | in the evening | last week |

1 I .... usually .... walk to school.
2 We are going to visit them ....
3 Dimitris went to bed at 12 o'clock ....
4 She watches TV ....

5 You didn't come to school ....
6 We drink milk for breakfast ....
7 Father isn't working ....
8 She wrote a letter to John ....

10 Put the verbs into the correct tense.

1 She always ..... goes ..... (go) to the park on Sundays.
2 I .... (buy) a new bicycle last week.
3 My family .... (go) to the theatre yesterday.
4 Ahmed .... (live) in London three years ago.
5 My mother .... (make) some coffee now.
6 Sam .... (go) to the circus tomorrow.
7 I .... (talk) on the telephone at the moment.
8 Sally always .... (help) her mother in the house.

GAME

When I ...

You are in two groups. A student from group A starts a story beginning with When I ... . Then a student from group B continues the story.

Group A Student 1: When I got home, I had a shower.
Group B Student 1: After I had a shower, I had lunch.
Group A Student 2: After I had lunch, I played football. etc.

11 Choose a word from the box to complete the story.

Last night Tom had 1) *dinner* and watched TV. Then he 2) .... to bed. At midnight he 3) .... a noise. He got out of bed and went to the 4) .... He looked outside and he 5) .... a monster. Tom was so scared that he 6) .... and hid under his 7) .... The monster got inside the house and started eating all the 8) .... When the monster got to Tom's bed, Tom started screaming. "It's OK, Tom," his mother said. "It was only a bad dream."

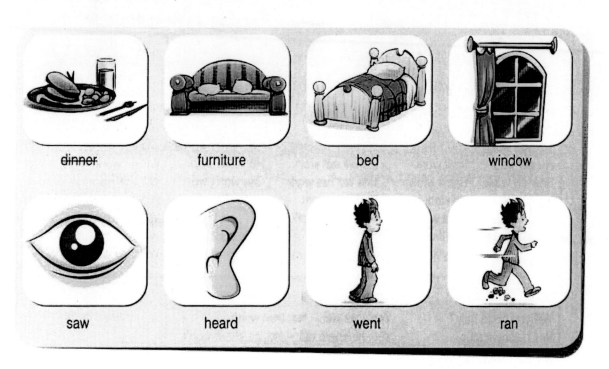

dinner   furniture   bed   window

saw   heard   went   ran

Writing Activity

Write a story that ends with the sentence: It was only a bad dream.

....

....

....

....

....

18

Simple Future

Listen and repeat. Then act out.

You will meet a beautiful girl. She will test you and she will check you. She will find out everything about you.

Great! Where will I meet her? In a park? In a pond?

In her biology class.

Affirmative		Negative		Interrogative
Long form	Short form	Long form	Short form	
I will work	I'll work	I will not work	I won't work	Will I work?
You will work	You'll work	You will not work	You won't work	Will you work?
He will work	He'll work	He will not work	He won't work	Will he work?
She will work	She'll work	She will not work	She won't work	Will she work?
It will work	It'll work	It will not work	It won't work	Will it work?
We will work	We'll work	We will not work	We won't work	Will we work?
You will work	You'll work	You will not work	You won't work	Will you work?
They will work	They'll work	They will not work	They won't work	Will they work?

Short answers

Will you go to Italy?	Yes, I/we will. – No, I/we won't.
Will he/she/it stop?	Yes, he/she/it will. – No, he/she/it won't.
Will they come to the party?	Yes, they will. – No, they won't.

We use the simple future:

- **to talk about things that may or may not happen in the future. We'll visit** Disney World **one day.**
- **with on-the-spot- decisions.** "We haven't got any sugar." "OK. I'll **go** and buy some."
- **with the verbs** hope, think, believe, expect, etc., the **expressions** I'm sure, I'm afraid, **etc. and the adverbs** probably, perhaps, **etc.**

1 Write the missing sentences.

1 I will go to Spain one day.
   I won't go to Spain one day.
   Will I go to Spain one day?

2 ....
   She won't come to the party.

3 We'll be late.
   ....

4 ....
   Will it snow?

110

2 What will Carl be like in 30 years' time? Write the questions and answers.

1 **(have long hair)** *Will he have long hair?*
  No, he won't.

2 **(have three children)** ....
  ....

3 **(have a car)** ....
  ....

4 **(wear glasses)** ....
  ....

5 **(have a beard and a moustache)** ....
  ....
  ....

6 **(have a cat)** ....
  ....

3 Complete the sentences. Use the verbs below with *will* or *won't*.

~~call~~   be   tell   miss   pass

1 A: Are you going to Tim's party?
  B: I don't know. I *will call* you later and let you know.

2 A: Hurry up. We .... the plane.
  B: Don't worry. We've got plenty of time.

3 A: Wendy .... the test.
  B: Why not?
  A: She doesn't study at all!

4 A: What's the matter, Jim?
  B: I'm afraid we .... late for the meeting.

5 A: I .... him anything again.
  B: Why not? Is everything OK?
  A: He's a big liar.

Simple Future

4 Match the sentences.

1 I haven't got my umbrella with me.
2 I'm hungry.
3 I can't find my pencil.
4 My head hurts.
5 I'm late for school.
6 I want to go to the concert, too.
7 The phone is ringing.
8 I haven't got any money on me.

a I'll give you one of mine.
b I'll drive you there.
c I'll answer it.
d I'll give you some.
e I'll bring you an aspirin.
f I'll give you mine.
g I'll make some sandwiches.
h I'll buy two tickets then.

GAME

What will happen to it? Be a fortune teller!

You are in two teams. Take turns to say what will happen to the items below. Each correct sentence wins a point. The team with the most points wins.

 egg
 brick
 chicken
 box
 tree
 wheel
 wool

 coffee beans
 butter
 wood
 glass
 metal
 bread
 milk

Team A Student 1: One – It will become a chicken.
Team B Student 1: Two – It will be part of a house.

Will vs be going to

We use the simple future:
- **for actions that will probably happen in the future**
  I will probably go to Spain next summer.
- **for on-the-spot-decisions**
  There's no tea left. I'll go and buy some.

We use be going to:
- **for plans and intentions**
  I bought two bags of flour because I am going to make a cake.
- **when there is evidence that something is going to happen in the future.**
  Be careful! You are going to fall into that hole.

112

5 Complete the dialogues.

1 clean my room / help you
A: *I'm going to clean my room.*
B: OK. *I'll help you* , then.

2 go to the greengrocer's / come with you
A: . . . .
B: OK. . . . . , then.

3 cook dinner / lay the table
A: . . . .
B: OK. . . . . , then.

4 mop the kitchen floor / clean windows
A: . . . .
B: OK. . . . . , then.

5 cut the grass / water the plants
A: . . . .
B: OK. . . . . , then.

6 wash the dishes / put them in the cupboard
A: . . . .
B: OK. . . . . , then.

Speaking Activity

What will life be like in the future? Put a tick (✓) or a cross (✗) and talk with your friend.

- go on holiday to the moon ☐   • have flying cars ☐   • live underwater ☐
- live on other planets ☐   • have T-shirts with computers on them ☐
- have no schools ☐   • have robots as teachers ☐   • have no electricity ☐

Student 1: I think in the future we'll go on holiday to the moon. What about you?
Student 2: Definitely. We'll also have flying cars.

Writing Activity

What will life be like in the future? Write.

In the future . . . .
. . . .
. . . .
. . . .
. . . .

1 Complete the text with the *past simple* form of the verbs in brackets.

Last Sunday we 1) ...*went*... (go) on a picnic in the country. My mum 2) .... (drive) the car. My dad 3) .... (sleep) all the way there because he was very tired. When we 4) .... (get) there, we 5) .... (run) straight to the river. We 6) .... (swim) for a long time and then we 7) .... (eat) our lunch. We 8) .... (leave) at six o'clock. We were tired but very happy. We had such a lovely time!

2 Read the text in Ex. 1 again and write the questions for the following answers.

1 When ...*did you go on a picnic*...?
Last Sunday.

2 Why .... all the way there?
Because he was tired.

3 When .... your lunch?
After our swim.

4 When ....?
At six o'clock.

3 Choose the correct item.

1 "There's no milk left."
"I ...... to the supermarket then."
A will go   B going to go
C went

2 When ...... back from school?
A did he come B did he came
C did come he

3 We've got tickets for the concert. We ......
the band live!
A saw   B will see
C are going to see

4 Did you ...... a music lesson yesterday?
A has   B have   C had

5 I forgot to feed the cat. I ...... it now.
A fed   B will feed
C am going to feed

6 I've got a cold. I ...... some hot chocolate.
A made   B will make
C am going to make

7 Tina ...... this story five years ago.
A wrote   B will write
C is going to write

8 "I like your new scarf."
"Really? I ...... you one like it then."
A will buy   B am going to buy
C bought

4 〔58〕 Listen and write a letter in each box.

• What did each person in Mr Smith's family choose to buy in the new supermarket?

Mr Smith [B]   Paula [ ]   Jenny [ ]

Alex [ ]   Harry [ ]   Mrs Smith [ ]

5 〔59〕 Song

Where did you go on Saturday?
I went to the seaside
I swam in the sea all day
I love the seaside!

What did you eat on Saturday?
I ate lots of ice cream
I ate lots of sandwiches, too
I love the seaside!

Who did you see on Saturday?
I saw my best friend
He came to the seaside with me!
We love the seaside!

Question Words

Match the questions to the answers.

ANIMAL FUN!!!

1 **Where** can you find an elephant?
2 **Why** did the cat put the letter 'M' in the fridge?
3 **How** do elephants talk to each other?
4 **What time** is it when an elephant sits on the fence?
5 **Who** is the bees' favourite singer?
6 **How many** bees do you need in a bee choir?
7 **What** is a dog's favourite food?
8 **When** does a dog go "moo"?

a **Because** it turns 'ice' into 'mice'.
b Anything that is on your plate.
c **By** 'elephone'!
d You don't have to find them. They're too big to lose.
e When it is learning a new language!
f Sting!
g A humdred!
h Time to fix the fence!

Moo...

1 Read and circle.

1 "**What** / **Who** is that?" "That's Mike."
2 "**Where** / **When** do you live?" "In Green Street."
3 "**How much** / **How many** is this CD?" "It's €15."
4 "**What** / **Who** is this?" "It's a pen."
5 "**How** / **How many** old are you?" "I'm 11."
6 "**What** / **What time** is it?" "It's half past eight."
7 "**Whose** / **Who** jacket is this?" "It's Sara's."

8 "**How much** / **How many** books have you got?" "Lots."
9 "**What** / **Why** are you happy?" "Because it's my birthday."
10 "**When** / **Where** is your birthday?" "On June 25th."
11 "**What** / **When** is the weather like?" "It's raining."

2 Complete the questions.

1 " _Why_ are you wearing a coat?"
"Because it's cold."

2 " .... is your party?" "On Saturday."

3 " .... money have you got?" "£10."

4 " .... is your school?" "It's near the station."

5 " .... brothers have you got?" "Two brothers."

6 " .... books have you got?" "Not many."

7 " .... is he?" "He's Mr Smith."

8 " .... are you reading that book?" "Because it's interesting."

9 " .... is the weather like?" "It's snowing."

10 " .... coat is this?" "It's Kurt's."

11 " .... does he come from?" "He comes from Brazil."

12 " .... is your birthday?" "In January."

13 " .... is it?" "7:30 pm."

14 " .... are you running?" "Because I'm late."

15 " .... sugar is there?" "One kilo."

16 " .... is he?" "In the kitchen."

17 " .... girls are there?" "12."

18 " .... are they doing?" "They're watching TV."

3 Complete the conversation with the correct question words.

Anna: Hi, Nick. 1) ... _What_ ... are you doing here?

Nick: I'm looking for a CD.

Anna: Oh look! I love this singer.

Nick: I don't know her. 2) .... is she?

Anna: She's Briony Spinks. She's great! I went to her concert.

Nick: Really? 3) .... was the concert?

Anna: It was last week.

Nick: 4) .... was it?

Anna: In the park.

Nick: 5) .... did you go with?

Anna: I went with my friends. We had a great time.

Nick: 6) .... people were at the concert?

Anna: Lots of people!

Nick: I'm going to buy her CD. 7) .... does it cost?

Anna: It's €20.

Nick: Great! Thanks, Anna!

Find someone...

Ask your friends and complete the table. Use question words.

Find someone ...	Name
1 whose father is a doctor.	
2 whose birthday is in spring.	
3 who is the same age as you.	
4 who lives near you.	
5 who has got two brothers or sisters.	

A: What does your father do, John?
B: He's a doctor.

Writing Activity

Tell your friend Cara about the following singer. Use the dialogue in Ex. 3 as a model.

Come
to the concert
on July 14th
at the Olympic
Stadium

Cara: Hi, ... What are you doing here?

. . . .:   I'm looking for a CD.

. . . . . .:   . . . .

. . . . . .:   . . . .

. . . . . .:   . . . .

. . . . . .:   . . . .

. . . . . .:   . . . .

. . . . . .:   . . . .

🎧 60 Listen and repeat. Then act out.

Adjectives describe nouns.
An elephant is a **wild** animal. (What kind of an animal is it? Wild.)

Remember: Adjectives remain the same in the plural.
He is a **clever** boy. They are **clever** boys.

Adjectives can go before a noun **or** after the verb 'to be'.
John is a **tall** man. John is **tall**.

1 **Put the adjectives in the correct place.**

1 He's a child. **(small)**
   He's a small child. . . . .

2 It's an elephant. **(big)**
   . . . .

3 It's a garden. **(beautiful)**
   . . . .

4 These are my sweets. **(favourite)**
   . . . .

5 She's got a smile. **(happy)**
   . . . .

6 He's got hair. **(short)**
   . . . .

2 **Rewrite the sentences as in the example:**

1 This is a red car.
   This car is red. . . . .

2 These are blue boots.
   . . . .

3 This is a long dress.
   . . . .

4 These are short trousers.
   . . . .

5 This is an easy exercise.
   . . . .

6 These are fat cats.
   . . . .

7 This is a hungry boy.
   . . . .

8 This is a nice girl.
   . . . .

Adjectives – Adverbs of manner

Listen and repeat. Then act out.

Adverbs of manner

Adverbs of manner describe verbs.
He is eating his lunch **quickly**. (How is he eating his lunch? Quickly.)

We form adverbs of manner by adding -ly to the adjective.
careful – carefully   loud – loudly   BUT   easy – easily

Some adjectives do not form their adverbs in the same way. These are:
good – **well**   fast – **fast**   hard – **hard**

---

3 Turn the following adjectives into adverbs.

1 loud – ..... *loudly* .....   4 fast – ....   7 quick – ....

2 good – ....   5 easy – ....   8 noisy – ....

3 careful – ....   6 hard – ....   9 happy – ....

4 Complete the sentences. Use the phrases from the box below.

~~his car slowly~~	French very well	happily together
the guitar badly	animals beautifully	his food fast

1 Tim drives ..... *his car slowly* ..... .   4 Khalid speaks ....

2 Nadia plays ....   5 Emma draws ....

3 Ivan usually eats ....   6 Anna and Carlos live ....

5 Rewrite the sentences as in the example:

1 She is a good dancer.
   She *dances well.* ....

2 You are a quick learner.
   You ....

3 Kelly is a hard worker.
   Kelly ....

4 Janet is a beautiful singer.
   Janet ....

6 Alex is at a summer camp. He wants to find some excuses to return home. Complete his letter.

Dear Mum,

Life here is great. All the children behave very 1) _well_ (good). Some girls talk very 2) .... (polite) to me. I share a room with a girl called Anna. She is very kind and she says that I sing 3) .... (beautiful)! Mrs Norris, the bus driver, drives very 4) .... (careful).

I'm having a good time here. See you soon.

Love,

Alex

What's the adverb?

You are in two teams. Your teacher gives you a verb and you must find an adverb which goes with it. Each correct answer wins one point. The team with the most points wins.

Teacher: walk
Team A student 1: slowly
Teacher: Correct. One point for Team A.

Writing Activity

You are at a summer camp and you are having a good time. Write a letter to your parents. Use Ex. 6 as a model.

Dear ....,

Life here is ....

....

....

....

....

....

1 Write *Who, Whose, What time, Where* or *Why*.

1 " *What time* is it?" "8:30 pm."

2 " . . . . car is this?" "It's my dad's."

3 " . . . . is she?" "She's my sister."

4 " . . . . is the milk?" "It's in the fridge."

5 " . . . . are you wearing your coat?" "Because it's cold outside."

6 " . . . . did she leave?" "At 6:20 am."

2 Find the mistakes and correct them.

1 How many sugar do you want? . . . *much* . . .

2 "Who is Bill?" "In the kitchen." . . . .

3 "When is the weather like?" "It's hot." . . . .

4 "Where is your birthday?" "In May." . . . .

5 "Who bike is this?" "Mine." . . . .

6 "Who are you late?" "Because I couldn't find a taxi." . . . .

3 Fill in the gaps as in the example.

 beautiful   beautifully   good   well

1 Lucy is a . . . . *beautiful* . . . . girl.

2 She paints . . . . *beautifully* . . . .

7 Renata plays tennis really . . . .

8 She's a . . . . tennis player.

 quick   quickly   bad   badly

3 George learns . . . .

4 He's a . . . . learner.

9 Isabel cooks very . . . .

10 She's a . . . . cook.

 careful   carefully   easy   easily

5 Ahmed is a . . . . driver.

6 He drives . . . .

11 This is an . . . . question.

12 I can answer it . . . .

4 [62] **Listen and write. There is one example.**

THE PARTY

1 When? ...last Saturday...

2 Whose birthday? ....

3 Where? ....

4 How many people? ....

5 What food? ....

6 Who took Sally? ....

5 [63]

The sun is shining brightly
What shall we do today?
Let's all go to the seaside
So we can swim and play

We're happy by the seaside
We're playing in the sun
Why don't you come and join us?
We're having lots of fun

The water's splashing gently
We're playing in the sea
We're swimming and we're sailing
We're laughing happily

Comparisons

Listen and repeat. Then act out.

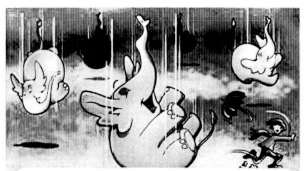

What's worse than it raining cats and dogs?
Raining elephants!

Which cows have the shortest tails?

The smallest ones.

Adjectives	Positive	Comparative	Superlative
one syllable	long	longer than	the longest
two syllables	happy	happier than	the happiest
more than two syllables	beautiful	more beautiful than	the most beautiful

We use comparative adjectives to compare *two* people, animals or things. We often use the word than after the comparative adjective.
I'm **taller than** you.
She is **more beautiful than** Wendy.

We use superlative adjectives to compare *three or more* people, animals or things. We use the word the before the superlative adjective.
I'm **the tallest** student in class.
She's **the most beautiful girl** in class.

Note: We use in for places after a superlative adjective.
She's the cleverest student **of** all.   She's the cleverest student **in** class.

Spelling

tall – tall**er** – tall**est**   small – small**er** – small**est**   strong – strong**er** – strong**est**

BUT

large – larg**er** – larg**est**   heavy – heav**ier** – heav**iest**   big – bi**gger** – bi**ggest**

Irregular form

good – **better** – **best**   much/many/a lot of – **more** – **most**   bad – **worse** – **worst**

1 Write the *comparative* and the *superlative* forms of the adjectives below.

1	tall	*taller*	*the tallest*
2	funny		
3	nice		
4	beautiful		
5	slim		
6	cold		
7	good		
8	easy		
9	careful		
10	bad		
11	fat		
12	long		

2 Look at the pictures, find the differences and complete the sentences.
Use: *fat*, *tall*, *old*, *long*, *big* and *happy*.

1 In picture A, the lizard is .... *longer than* .... the lizard in picture B.
2 In picture B, the girl is .... the girl in picture A.
3 In picture B, the boy is .... the boy in picture A.
4 In picture A, the woman is .... the woman in picture B.
5 In picture B, the giraffe is .... the giraffe in picture A.
6 In picture A, the hippo is .... the hippo in picture B.

3 Complete the sentences. Then write *yes* or *no*.

Name	Height	Age	
Aya	140 cm	9 years	8 months
Jill	145 cm	10 years	1 month
Luke	147 cm	10 years	3 months
Nora	142 cm	9 years	6 months
Pedro	143 cm	9 years	4 months
Khalid	146 cm	10 years	7 months

1 Pedro is o *lder* than Luke. *no*
2 Nora is t............ than Aya.
3 Jill is o............ than Pedro and Nora.
4 Khalid is t............ than Luke.
5 Luke is o............ than Khalid.
6 Aya is t............ than Pedro.
7 Nora is o............ than Pedro.
8 Luke is t............ than Jill and Khalid.
9 Khalid is o............ than Luke and Jill.

4 Read and write.

I usually live in a house or on a farm. I am 1) .... *smaller* .... (small) than a rabbit but I'm 2) .... (big) than a snail. I am 3) .... (slow) than a cat but I'm 4) .... (clever) than a rabbit. I love cheese!

What am I?
I'm a 5) ....

5 Complete the dialogues.

1 A: Which countries did you visit last summer?
   B: England, Italy and Spain.
   A: Which did you like .... *the best* .... (good)?
   B: Italy. It's .... (beautiful) country in the world.

2 A: Let's buy a new computer.
   B: How much is .... (cheap) one?
   A: I don't know. We can ask.

3 A: You must take some warm clothes with you.
   B: Why?
   A: It's .... (cold) place in England.

4 A: I want to buy a house in Madrid.
   B: Are you sure? It's .... (expensive) city in Spain!

5 A: How was your Maths test?
   B: It was .... (bad) of all. I couldn't answer anything.

6 A: Tony is very tall.
   B: Yes. He's .... (tall) boy in our class.

7 A: I want to buy a Porsche!
   B: Why?
   A: It's .... (fast) car in the world!

6 Complete the sentences with *of*, *in* or *than*.

1 My room is larger *than* yours.
2 The white car is the fastest .... the three cars.
3 Watching TV is more interesting .... listening to the radio.

4 He is the cleverest boy .... his class.
5 She is richer .... me.
6 They are the fastest runners .... all.
7 Summer is hotter .... winter.
8 Tom is the oldest .... all.

7 Complete the sentences.

1 My car is *faster than* yours. (**fast**)
2 She is the .... all. (**thin**)
3 It is the .... book of the three. (**interesting**)
4 Paula is .... Fatimah. (**short**)
5 Maths is .... History. (**difficult**)

6 She is the .... her class. (**pretty**)
7 Tim is .... Harry. (**happy**)
8 Dimitris is .... Ivan. (**careful**)
9 Don is the .... student .... the class. (**lazy**)
10 Meera is .... Nora. (**beautiful**)

8 Complete the sentences.

1 The red dress is *the most expensive* of all. (**expensive**)

2 John is .... than Jim. (**tall**)

3 A horse is .... than a cat. (**big**)

4 Tina is .... than her brother. (**short**)

5 Luigi is .... than Anton. (**fat**)

6 Sally is .... girl in the class. (**beautiful**)

9   Correct the sentences.

1   I am tallest than you.   *taller*
2   She's the more beautiful girl I know.
3   Are you older of your brother?
4   I've got longest hair than you.
5   Derek is thiner than me.

Speaking Activity

Work with your friend and complete the table.

Who ...	me	my friend
• is a better student?	....	....
• is better at sports?	....	....
• is taller?	....	....
• is older?	....	....
• has got shorter hair?	....	....
• has got longer arms?	....	....

Writing Activity

Write about you and your friend. Use the information from the Speaking Activity.

Me and my Friend

by ....

My name is .... My friend's name is ....

....

....

....

....

And – But – Or – Because

🎧 65 **Listen and repeat. Then act out.**

I'm short and fat.

I'm fat too but I'm tall.

I'm not short or fat.

You're different because these are special mirrors!

We use and to join two similar ideas.
He is tall. He is thin. → He is tall **and** thin.

We use but to join two different ideas.
I can dance. I can't sing. → I can dance **but** I can't sing.

We use or to join two possibilities.
I can come now. I can come tomorrow. → I can come now **or** tomorrow.

We use because to give a reason.
Why are you late? **Because** my car didn't work.

---

1 **Read and complete the sentences with *and* or *but*.**

1 I wanted to go skiing
 a) ....*but*.... I didn't have any skis.
 b) ....*and*.... mountain climbing.

2 I can play tennis
 a) .... my brother is better than me.
 b) .... volleyball.

3 The show was interesting
 a) .... it was very long.
 b) .... I liked it.

4 I've got her phone number
 a) .... her email address.
 b) .... I don't want to call her.

5 I've got a bike
 a) .... I can't ride it.
 b) .... rollerblades.

And – But – Or – Because

2 Join the sentences. Use *and*.

1 Harry is kind. He is friendly.
2 The food was cheap. It was delicious.
3 Martha can play football. She can play basketball.
4 I bought a hat. I bought a scarf.
5 The play was long. It was boring.
6 Judy is a mother. She is a doctor.

3 Choose the correct item.

1 He's rich. He's got a villa ..... a yacht.
   (A) and   B but   C or

2 She's American ..... Canadian. I'm not sure.
   A and   B but   C or

3 I've got a sister ..... I haven't got a brother.
   A and   B but   C or

4 I'm so angry ..... my brother took my bike.
   A and   B because   C or

5 Which dress should I buy? The red ..... the blue one?
   A and   B but   C or

6 Jill is rude ..... mean! I don't like her at all!
   A and   B but   C or

7 He left the party early ..... got home late.
   A and   B but   C or

8 Will you come with us ..... will you stay here and watch TV?
   A and   B but   C or

9 I want to go shopping ..... I haven't got any money.
   A and   B but   C or

10 "Why did you buy all these balloons?"
   "..... I'm having a party tomorrow!"
   A Because   B But   C Or

4 Correct the sentences.

1 Has she got dark hair **but** fair hair?   ..... or .....
2 I'm late **or** I missed the train.
3 Tina is rich **or** famous.
4 I can't ride a horse **because** I can ride a bike.
5 I can sing **but** play the guitar at the same time.
6 Are you coming **and** are you staying here?
7 I'm crying **or** I'm very sad.
8 She's here **or** she doesn't want to talk to you.

130

Brain GYM

How many excuses to the following question can you find in 2 minutes? Compare them with your friends.

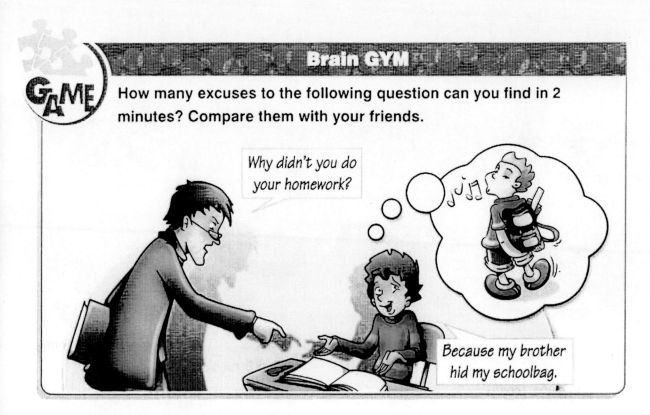

Writing Activity

In groups, decide on and write the six best excuses for not doing your homework.

....

....

....

....

....

....

1 Look at the pictures and complete the sentences.

1
2
3
4

5
6
7
8

1 Zahra ....*is taller than*.... Kelly. **(tall)**

2 It is .... in Finland ....
   in England. **(cold)**

3 John is .... his brother
   Peter. **(young)**

4 The brown sweater is ....
   the blue one. **(expensive)**

5 Buddy is .... Blackie. **(thin)**

6 The pink rabbit is ....
   the yellow one. **(hungry)**

7 My sandwich is .... yours.
   (big)

8 The Glamour Hotel is ....
   the Grand Hotel. **(modern)**

2 Complete the text with *and*, *or*, *but*, *because*.

Dear Sue,

   Greetings from sunny Spain. It's very hot 1) ....*and*.... sunny here. The hotel is
excellent 2) .... it's very small. There are only ten rooms. The people here are very
kind 3) .... friendly. Guess what! I met a girl. Her name is Carla. She is from Brazil
4) .... Argentina. I'm not sure.

   I want to buy Mum a hat 5) .... a T-shirt. Which one do you think she'll like more?
Oh yes, I almost forgot. I want to send Frank an email 6) .... I lost his email address.
Can you send it to me, please?

   I have to run now 7) .... I am going to meet Carla in five minutes 8) ....
I don't want to be late.

Talk to you soon.

Bob

3 **Write sentences as in the example:**

1 the Sahara Desert / be / dry place / in Africa
   The Sahara Desert is the driest
   place in Africa.

2 Mount Everest / be / high mountain / in world
   . . . .

3 the Nile / be / long river / in world
   . . . .

4 Judy / be / pretty girl / I know

5 Athens / be / big city / in Greece

6 George / be / careful drive / I know
   . . . .

4 [66] **Listen and write. There is one example.**

The Animal Park

When?	1	*Friday*
How many kinds of animals?	2	
Biggest animal?	3	
Favourite animal?	4	
Favourite animal's food?	5	
Name of Animal Park?	6	Park

5 [67]

You're a fast runner
But I can run faster
I am the fastest
I'm faster than you

You're a good singer
But I can sing better
I'm the best singer
I'm better than you

Anything you can do
I can do better
I can do anything
Better than you

1 Underline the correct word.

He / Him is 10 years old.

1 I / Me am from England.

2 He can't do it. Help he / him, please.

3 Where's Nadia? Can you see she / her?

4 We / Us can go to the cinema.

5 Give they / them these pens, please.

Points: ——
5x2   10

2 Look at the pictures and write questions and answers.

Has he got................. a bike?
No, he hasn't. He's got a car.......

1 .... a piano?

2 .... a parrot?

3 .... a TV?

4 .... a kite?

5 .... short hair?

Points: ——
5x2   10

3 Put the words in the correct order to make sentences as in the example:

from / I / London / am
I am from London...............

1 home / she / at / isn't

2 a / Nadia / ride / can't / horse

3 fly / you / a / kite / can?

4 I / short / got / haven't / hair

5 sea / they / swim / the / can / in

Points: ——
5x2   10

4 Circle the correct word.

a /(some) tea

1 a / some cheese

2 a / some book

3 a / some juice

4 a / some water

5 a / some boy

6 a / some girl

7 a / some bread

8 a / some flag

9 a / some honey

10 a / some milk

11 a / some bird

Points: ——
11x2   22

5 Look at the pictures and complete the sentences.

This is my *dress* .　　1 ...... are ....　　2 ...... is a ....

3 ...... are ....　　4 ...... are ....　　5 ...... is a ....

(Points: ——
　5x2　10)

6 Write the plurals.

box – *boxes*	5 bus –	10 butterfly – ....
1 parrot –	6 glass –	11 boy – ....
2 banana –	7 watch –	12 baby – ....
3 ox –	8 child –	13 thief – ....
4 dolphin –	9 potato –	14 foot – ....

(Points: ——
　14x2　28)

7 Correct the sentences.

Can I have a ~~jar~~ of milk, please?　　*carton*

1 They **are** dark hair.　　..............
2 **Those** is my new scarf.　　..............
3 Can I have **a** water, please?　　..............
4 Two **cans** of bread, please.　　..............
5 Are **them** your friends?　　..............

(Points: ——
　5x2　10)

(Total: ——
　　100)

1 Circle the correct word.

He's got a cat.
It's he / **(his)** cat.

1 He's got flowers.
They're **his** / him .

2 She's got an umbrella.
It's **her** / hers .

3 We've got shorts.
They are **our** / ours shorts.

4 I've got a guitar.
It's **my** / mine .

5 They've got a TV.
It's **their** / theirs .

(Points: —— / 5x1 5)

2 Write the plurals.

woman – ....women....
1 goose – ....
2 leaf – ....
3 sheep – ....

4 mouse – ....
5 roof – ....
6 table – ....
7 bus – ....

8 child – ....
9 knife – ....
10 dress – ....
11 video – ....

(Points: —— / 11x2 22)

3 Read and tick (✓).

This is John's car. [✓]
This is Johns' car. [ ]

1 He is ten years old. [ ]
He has got ten years old. [ ]

2 This are men's shirts. [ ]
These are men's shirts. [ ]

3 Mike has got a new bike. [ ]
Mike have got a new bike. [ ]

4 Bring two knives, please. [ ]
Bring two knifes, please. [ ]

5 Can you buy a carton of bread? [ ]
Can you buy a loaf of bread? [ ]

(Points: —— / 5x2 10)

4 Write *some* or *any*.

There is ....*some*.... cake on the table.

1 There aren't .... tomatoes in the fridge.

2 Is there .... sugar in the jar?

3 There are .... children in the park.

4 Are there .... books on the table?

5 There isn't .... butter in the fridge.

6 There are .... girls in the classroom.

7 Are there .... birds in the trees?

8 There aren't .... bikes in the street.

Points: ——
8x3   24

5 Look at the picture and write questions and answers.

cakes
Are there any cakes .... ?
No, there aren't ....

1 strawberries
.... ?
....

2 meat
.... ?
....

3 apples
.... ?
....

4 cheese
.... ?
....

5 milk
.... ?
....

6 oranges
.... ?
....

Points: ——
6x4   24

6 Correct the sentences.

~~That~~ are oxen.   ....*Those*....

1 Can I have a **carton** of soup, please?   ....

2 **They're** house is big.   ....

3 The **childrens'** room is very small.   ....

4 **They** are five boys in my class.   ....

5 The **boy's** names are Jack and Bill.   ....

Points: ——
5x3   15

Total: ——
100

1 Correct the sentences.

Their my friends.   they're

1 Look at **he**. He's so funny!
2 Martha has got two **babys**.
3 The **mens'** shirts are over there.
4 **Your** Mike's brother. Right?
5 This T-shirt isn't **my**.

Points: ——
5x4   20

2 Complete the text with the *present continuous*.

This is me and my family. We are at the park. My sister
....*is painting*.... **(paint)** a picture. Can you see my
two brothers? They 1) .... **(ride)**
their bikes. My mum 2) .... **(sit)**
on a bench. She 3) .... **(read)** a book.
Look at my dad. He 4) .... **(write)**
an email. Can you see me? I'm under the tree. I
5) .... **(play)** my guitar.

Points: ——
5x3   15

3 Complete the text with the *present simple*.

This is Anna. She ......*lives*.... **(live)** in a big house.
Anna 1) .... **(get up)** early every
morning. She 2) .... **(brush)**
her teeth, 3) .... **(have)**
a shower and 4) .... **(catch)** the
bus to school. After school, Anna and her brother Sean
5) .... **(go)** swimming. They love
swimming!

Points: ——
5x3   15

4 Complete the questions and answers.

_Do_ they like fish? No, _they don't_ .

1 .... you want some juice? Yes, ...

2 .... Fatimah sleeping? No, ...

3 .... they doing their homework? Yes, ...

4 .... Pete and Sue like pizza? No, ...

5 .... Carmen help her mother? No, ...

Points: ——
5x3   15

5 Choose the correct item.

He ...... milk for breakfast.
(A) always drinks
B drinks always
C always drink

1 We usually ...... at home in the evening.
A stay
B are staying
C stays

2 She ...... lunch at the moment.
A cooks
B is cook
C is cooking

3 Why ...... late?
A you always are
B are you always
C always are you

4 They ...... to Spain on holiday.
A often goes
B are often going
C often go

5 Listen! The birds ...... !
A are singing
B is singing
C sing

Points: ——
5x4   20

6 Complete the text with the *present continuous* or the *present simple*.

John usually ...... _goes_ ...... **(go)** to the park every Sunday. He
1) .... **(meet)** his friends there and they usually
2) .... **(play)** football. Today John isn't at the park.
He is at home. He 3) .... **(help)** his father. They
4) .... **(cook)** dinner for all the family. It's John's
mother's birthday and they 5) .... **(have)** a surprise
birthday party.

Points: ——
5x3   15

Total: ——
100

1 Read and match.

Has she got a new car?

1 Are you Tom's sister?
2 Have we got a new teacher?
3 Can you carry my bag for me?
4 Is Emma's mum a doctor?
5 Can you stand on one leg?

A Yes. I am. Are you his friend George?
B Sorry. I can't. It's very heavy.
C Yes, I can. Look!
D No she isn't. Nora's mum is a doctor.
E No, she hasn't. She's got a new motorbike.
F Yes, we have. His name is Mr Robbins.

Points: ——
5x2   10

2 Underline the correct word.

This book is **my / mine**.

1 Mr Smith is **their / theirs** teacher.
2 **There / It** is a vase on the table.
3 This is **our / ours** house.
4 **My / Mine** dog is black and white.

5 Can I have a **glass / loaf** of water?
6 The black skirt is **her / hers**.
7 This is John's book. It's **his / her**.
8 This car is **their / theirs**.
9 Dr Black is **her / hers** doctor.

Points: ——
9x3   27

3 Put the verbs into the *present simple* or the *present continuous*.

Helen: Hello, Nadia. What .... *are you doing* .... (you/do)?
Nadia: I 1) .... (cook) dinner.
Helen: But you 2) .... (never/cook) dinner on Saturdays.
　　　 You 3) .... (always/eat) out.
Nadia: Not today. My grandson Matthew 4) .... (be) here. He
　　　 5) .... (fix) my garage door. I 6) .... (make) his
　　　 favourite meal, lemon chicken.
Helen: Lemon chicken? Can I come, too?

Points: ——
6x3   18

4 Write the opposites.

Don't talk!　　　　　*Talk!*

1 Open the window!　.............
2 Don't stamp your feet!　.............

3 Stand up!　.............
4 Make a noise!　.............
5 Stop!　.............

Points: ——
5x3   15

5 Look at the picture and circle the correct word.

There is a poster (above) / on the bed.

1 There is a book **under** / **on** the bed.

2 There is an umbrella **under** / **in** the bed.

3 There is a desk **next to** / **behind** the bed.

4 There are two chairs **behind** / **in front of** the desk.

5 There is a box **opposite** / **between** the two chairs.

(Points: ——
 5x3   15)

6 Look at the picture and complete the text. Use: *in*, *between*, *in front of*, *next to*, *above*, *on*.

This is Falls Street. There are a lot of shops ...... *in* ...... Falls Street. There is a supermarket
1) .... the bank and the greengrocer's. There is a nice café 2) ....
the greengrocer's. Can you see Mr Smith? His house is 3) .... ours. Can you see
the man 4) .... the bank? That's my dad. He works there. What's my dog, Spot,
doing 5) .... that car? Spot, come here!

(Points: ——
 5x3   15)

(Total: ——
      100)

Revision 5 (Units 1-10)

1 Underline the correct word.

Tina is **my** / mine sister.
1 He's got five **box** / **boxes**.
2 There **is** / **are** two men in the garden.
3 That skirt is **her** / **hers**.
4 Is there **some** / **any** cola left?
5 **My** / **Mine** brother is tall.
6 This is **Sue** / **Sue's** bike.
7 That is **your** / **yours** pen.
8 These are **our** / **ours** bags.
9 This is **Bob** / **Bob's** train.
10 There aren't **some** / **any** plates on the table.

(Points: ——
  10x2   20)

2 Put the verbs into the *present simple* or the *present continuous*.

The children .... *are playing* .... (play) outside now.
1 He sometimes .... (go) to the cinema.
2 I .... (do) my homework at the moment.
3 I .... (read) the newspaper every morning.
4 I .... (eat) my dinner now.
5 She usually .... (read) a book before she .... (go) to bed.
6 He .... (write) an email to his friend every night.

(Points: ——
  6x3   18)

3 Choose the correct item.

Our lesson begins .... 9 o'clock.
A in   **B** on   ©at
1 My birthday is .... November.
A in   **B** on   **C** at
2 I usually go jogging .... the afternoon.
A in   **B** on   **C** at
3 The shops are not open .... Sundays.
A in   **B** on   **C** at
4 What fruit do you eat .... winter?
A in   **B** on   **C** at
5 His birthday party is .... Saturday.
A in   **B** on   **C** at
6 I have a shower .... I get dressed.
A before   **B** after   **C** now
7 Foxes hunt .... night.
A in   **B** on   **C** at
8 Paul's birthday is .... July 4th.
A in   **B** on   **C** at
9 My guitar lesson is .... Tuesday.
A in   **B** on   **C** at
10 What are you doing here .... midnight?
A in   **B** on   **C** at
11 I brush my teeth .... I have lunch.
A before   **B** after   **C** now
12 Mother's Day is .... March.
A in   **B** on   **C** at
13 My holidays begin .... August 15th.
A in   **B** on   **C** at

(Points: ——
  13x2   26)

4 Look at the picture and answer the questions. Use the prepositions in the box.

in   behind   on   under   next to   between   above

Where's the woman?

She's ...*in*.... the house.

1 Where's the man?

He's .... the window.

2 Where's the horse?

It's .... the man.

3 Where's the bird?

It's .... the house.

4 Where are the trees?

They're .... the house.

5 Where's the rabbit?

It's .... the trees.

6 Where's the cat?

It's .... the roof.

Points: ——
6x3   18

5 Complete the questions and write the answers.

...How much... milk is there?	. a carton.
1 .... apples are there?	....
2 .... lemonade is there?	....
3 .... jam is there?	....
4 .... cheese is there?	....
5 .... glasses are there?	....
6 .... cereal is there?	....

Points: ——
6x3   18

Total: ——
100

1 Underline the correct word.

The cat is **hers** / her.

1 The car is **your** / **yours**.

2 **These** / **This** books are mine.

3 Is there **some** / **any** milk?

4 Can I have **a** / **an** egg?

5 I want a **jar** / **loaf** of coffee.

6 There is **some** / **any** water in the vase.

(Points: ——)
(6x2   12)

2 Complete the sentences. Use *There is* / *There are* or *How much* / *How many*.

..*There are*.. some eggs in the basket.

1 .... some butter in the fridge.

2 .... knives are there on the table?

3 .... popcorn is there in the box?

4 .... some birds in the tree.

5 .... money do you have?

6 .... a mouse under the bed.

7 .... horses are there in the field?

8 .... some apples in the fridge.

9 .... some flowers in the vase.

10 .... books have you got?

(Points: ——)
(10x2   20)

3 Write the sentences. Use *be going to*.

(play/football)

..They are going to..
.play football.......

1 (clean/the windows)

....
....

2 (make/a cake)

....
....

3 (feed/the baby)

....
....

4 (play/tennis)

....
....

5 (take/photos)

....
....

(Points: ——)
(5x4   20)

4 Look at the picture and fill in the correct preposition.

There is a plant _on_ the table. There is a phone 1) .... the book and the plant. There is a picture 2) .... the table. There is a cat 3) ...... the table. There are some letters 4) .... the floor. There is a shopping bag 5) .... the chair. There is a newspaper 6) .... the shopping bag. 7) ...... the chair there is an umbrella.

Points: ——
7x3   21

5 Put the verbs into the *present simple* or the *present continuous*.

Kate: Hello, Peter. What .... *are you doing* .... (you/do)?

Peter: Nothing much. I 1) .... (sit) here with my dog, Rex.

Kate: 2) .... (you/want) to take Rex for a walk on the beach?

Peter: No, Rex 3) .... (not/like) the sea! He 4) .... (be) afraid of the water.

Kate: 5) .... (he/like) going to the park?

Peter: Yes, he 6) .... Let's go to the park!

Points: ——
6x2   12

6 Write the sentences.

the boys / play the drums
(love)

.The.boys love.......
.playing.the.drums..

1   John / go to the dentist's
(hate)

....
....

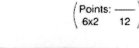

2   Ann / do the housework
(not want)

....
....

3   the children / play with their toys **(like)**

....
....

4   the girls / go to the beach **(like)**

....
....

5   Erica / eat ice cream **(love)**

....
....

Points: ——
5x3   15

Total: ——
100

Revision 7 (Units 1-14)

1 Choose the correct item.

Look at .... ! He's so tall!

A he   **(B)** him   **C** his

1 ...... is from Japan.

A She   **B** Her   **C** Hers

2 Are there ...... letters for me?

A some   **B** any   **C** a

3 ...... a car in the street?

A Is there   **B** Are there   **C** Is it

4 What do you do ...... the afternoon?

A in   **B** on   **C** at

5 We ...... to the theatre on Fridays.

A are sometimes go

B go sometimes

C sometimes go

6 You ...... drink milk. It's good for you.

A must   **B** mustn't   **C** may

7 ...... some eggs in the fridge.

A There are   **B** They are   **C** There is

8 ...... sugar do you want?

A How   **B** How much   **C** How many

9 I like ...... fishing.

A go   **B** going   **C** to going

10 Lucy ...... in a big hotel.

A is going to stay

B is going stay

C is go to stay

$\left(\begin{array}{c} \text{Points: } \underline{\quad} \\ \text{10x2} \quad \text{20} \end{array}\right)$

2 Put the verbs into the *present simple* or the *present continuous*.

Ann: Where is John? .... *Is he playing* ... **(he/play)** football?

Sally: No, he usually 1) .... **(play)** football but his back 2) .... **(hurt)** today.

Ann: So what 3) .... **(he/do)**?

Sally: He's in the living room. He 4) .... **(lie)** on the sofa and he 5) .... **(watch)** the football match on TV.

$\left(\begin{array}{c} \text{Points: } \underline{\quad} \\ \text{5x3} \quad \text{15} \end{array}\right)$

3 Look at the picture and complete the sentences. Use *in*, *on*, *under*, *between* or *behind*.

There's a bag .... *on* .... the bed.

1 The table is .... the bed and the wardrobe.

2 There are two blue socks .... the table.

3 There is a brown cat .... the computer.

4 There is a white cat .... the wardrobe.

5 There is a poster .... the wall.

$\left(\begin{array}{c} \text{Points: } \underline{\quad} \\ \text{5x4} \quad \text{20} \end{array}\right)$

146

4 Choose the correct sentence.

You want to watch a TV programme. What do you say?

(A) May I watch this TV programme?

B Do I have to watch this TV programme?

1 Your friend is very thirsty. What do you say?

A Shall I bring you a glass of water?

B Must I bring you a glass of water?

2 Your father is talking to you about your new school. You do not want to wear a school uniform. What do you say?

A May I wear a uniform?

B Do I have to wear a uniform?

3 It's very cold and the window is open. What do you say?

A Do I have to close the window?

B May I close the window?

4 Your mum is carrying some bags. They're heavy. What do you say?

A Shall I help you, Mum?

B Do I have to help you, Mum?

5 You want to use your teacher's dictionary to look up a word. What do you say?

A May I use your dictionary?

B Shall I use your dictionary?

Points: ——
5x5   25

5 Write the questions and answers.

(Mark/at the circus/ yesterday)

. Was Mark at the .
. circus yesterday? .
. Yes, he was. . . . .

1 **(the boys/at the park/ yesterday evening)**

2 **(Mary/at the zoo/last Sunday)**

3 **(Juan/in London/last summer)**

4 **(the girls/at a party/ yesterday afternoon)**

5 **(Cara/at the theatre/last night)**

Points: ——
5x4   20

Total: ——
100

1 **Circle the correct item.**

There are (some) / any glasses on the table.
1 Is there **some** / **any** milk left?
2 **How much** / **How many** honey have you got?
3 **How much** / **How many** lemons do we need?

4 **How much** / **How many** milk do we need?
5 There is **some** / **any** cheese in the pie.
6 There aren't **some** / **any** apples in the bag.
7 **How much** / **How many** pens have you got?

Points: ——
7x2   14

2 **Join the sentences. Use *before* or *after*.**

I always have breakfast. I go to school.
I always have breakfast before I go to school.

1 We wash the dishes. We have dinner.
. . . .

2 He always has a shower. He gets dressed.
. . . .

3 Janet always reads a book. She goes to sleep.
. . . .

4 Mike always brushes his teeth. He has a meal.
. . . .

Points: ——
4x3   12

3 **Look at the picture and complete the text. Use the correct preposition from the list.**

next to	~~on~~	in front of	above
in	behind	between	under

Look at this pet shop. There is a goldfish bowl ...*on*... the table. There is a goldfish 1) . . . . the bowl. The bowl is 2) . . . . a cat and a box of cat biscuits. There is a rabbit 3) . . . . the table. Can you see the plants 4) . . . . the table? There is a ball 5) . . . . them. Can you see the shelf 6) . . . . the plants? There's a mouse there. It's 7) . . . . the cat food.

Points: ——
7x3   21

4 Choose the correct item.

Tony .... fishing every weekend.
A is going   (**B**) goes
C is going to go

1 Liz .... her new dress at the party next Saturday.
A wearing   **B** wears
C is going to wear

2 I .... a cake. Come and see!
A am making   **B** make
C going to make

3 We ...... Mark's birthday on Saturday.
A celebrating   **B** celebrate
C are going to celebrate

4 Mum .... lunch right now.
A is cooking   **B** cooks
C is going to cook

5 How often .... tennis?
A do you playing   **B** do you play
C do you going to play

Points: ——
5x3   15

5 Underline the correct word.

<u>Can I</u> / **Must I** go to the zoo, please? All my friends are going!
1 You **can** / **must** be kind to your cousin. She doesn't know anyone else here.
2 I **can** / **could** walk when I was one year old.
3 **Do I have to** / **May I** come with you? I'm so tired.

4 **Can I** / **Do I have to** go to the cinema? There's a film on I want to see.
5 **Must I** / **May I** leave the table, please?
6 You **can't** / **mustn't** go to the cinema tonight.
7 You **mustn't** / **may not** tell lies. It's bad.
8 **Shall I** / **Must I** make you a cup of tea?

Points: ——
8x3   24

6 Write *am*, *is*, *are*, *was* or *were*.

I ...*am*... at school right now.
1 Zahra .... at a party last night.
2 It .... hot today.
3 You and Ahmed .... late yesterday morning.

4 We .... at the cinema at the moment.
5 They .... in Rome last month.
6 I .... at home last night.
7 He .... at his grandma's last Sunday.

Points: ——
7x2   14

Total: ——
100

Revision 9 (Units 1-18)

1 Fill in the correct preposition.

On Sundays the children get up 1) .... 10 o'clock 2) .... the morning. They watch TV and then they go to the park. 3) .... the afternoon they usually go to the cinema. They go to bed 4) .... 9 o'clock 5) .... night.

(Points: ——)
(5x4   20)

2 Look at the picture and complete the sentences. Use *in front of*, *behind*, *between*, *next to*, *opposite*.

There's a purple car .. *in front of* .. a green lorry.

1 There's a yellow car .... the green lorry and a pink lorry.
2 There's a taxi .... the pink lorry.
3 There's a man .... a boy.
4 The boy and the man are standing .... the bus stop.

(Points: ——)
(4x1   4)

3 Mr Harmer is telling his son what he must or mustn't do. Fill in the gaps with *must* or *mustn't*.

You .. *mustn't* .. forget to do your homework.

1 You .... drink your milk.
2 You .... come home late.
3 You .... be so noisy!
4 You .... remember to feed the rabbit.

5 You .... leave your room untidy.
6 You .... wash your hands before you eat dinner.
7 You .... fight with your sister.
8 You .... help your mother.
9 You .... visit your grandparents.

(Points: ——)
(9x2   18)

4 **Underline the correct item.**

She **sleeps** / <u>**is sleeping**</u> now.

1 They **go** / **went** to the cinema last night.

2 They want **to visit** / **visiting** Greece next year.

3 Look at her! She **is crying** / **cried**.

4 He **is waking** / **woke** up late yesterday.

5 She loves **making** / **make** cakes.

6 We **are going to visit** / **visit** our grandparents tomorrow.

7 Look! That cat **climbs** / **is climbing** up the tree!

8 We **didn't** / **don't** go to school yesterday.

9 He **had** / **is having** a bath at the moment.

Points: ——
9x2   18

5 **Complete the sentences with: *have to* or *don't have to*.**

- wash the dishes ✗
- serve the meals ✓
- wear a uniform ✓
- work in the mornings ✗
- be polite to customers ✓
- get up early ✗

You ...*don't have to*... wash the dishes.

1 You .... serve the meals.

2 You .... wear a uniform.

3 You .... work in the mornings.

4 You .... be polite to customers.

5 You .... get up early.

Points: ——
5x4   20

6 **Match. Then write.**

b	bring you some lemons
1	be back tonight
2	be sunny tomorrow
3	go to a party tonight
4	buy a video camera

a come with you

b make a lemon pie

c take a video of her baby

d have a picnic

e visit them

A: Jenny ...*is going to bring you some lemons*....

B: Really? I .*'ll make a lemon pie, then*...........

1 A: Monica and Karl ....

B: Really? I ....

2 A: It ....

B: Really? We ....

3 A: I ....

B: Really? I ....

4 A: Meera ....

B: Really? She ....

Points: ——
4x5   20

Total: ——
100

1 Write the sentences in the plural.

This is a ball.
These are balls.

1 That is a fox.

. . . .

2 This is a baby.

. . . .

3 That is a bed.

. . . .

4 That is a bus.

. . . .

5 This is a horse.

. . . .

Points: —— 5x2 10

2 Underline the correct item.

John wants **some** / **any** bananas.

1 Have you got **some** / **any** money?
2 How **much** / **many** butter is there?
3 He came **at** / **on** five o'clock.
4 There are **some** / **any** children in the park.
5 Are there **some** / **any** apples left?
6 How **much** / **many** oranges are there?
7 What do you do **in** / **on** the summer?
8 I want to **go** / **going** to the cinema.
9 Do you like **swimming** / **to swimming**?

Points: —— 9x1 9

3 Fill in the correct word from the box.

mine   your   ~~his~~   hers   its   ours   her   their

The radio is . . . *his* . . . . **(Tom)**

1 When is . . . . birthday? **(you)**
2 This book is . . . . **(I)**
3 . . . . house is big. **(Pedro & Isabel)**
4 These pens are . . . . **(Aya & I)**
5 These flowers are . . . . **(Mother)**
6 . . . . hair is very long. **(Camila)**
7 That is . . . . bed. **(cat)**

Points: —— 7x2 14

4 Put the verbs into the *present simple* or the *present continuous*.

Bob . . . . *is washing* . . . . **(wash)** his car at the moment.

1 My sister . . . . **(eat)** her dinner now.
2 I always . . . . **(do)** my homework in the evening.
3 Mother usually . . . . **(do)** the housework at the weekend.
4 Khalid . . . . **(tidy)** his room now.
5 They usually . . . . **(go)** on holiday in August.
6 Jane always . . . . **(go)** to bed early.
7 My dad usually . . . . **(sleep)** in the afternoon.
8 He . . . . **(write)** an email at present.

Points: —— 8x1 8

5 Complete the text with the correct preposition.

My name is Peter. I live *in* New York. I have an apartment 1) .... the 8th floor of an apartment block. My friend Sue lives in an flat 2) .... mine 3) .... the 9th floor. Sue and I like getting together 4) .... Sundays. We usually meet 5) .... one o'clock 6) .... the afternoon and have lunch together. Then we go for a walk or stay at home and watch TV. 7) .... the summer we usually have our lunch 8) .... Central Park. It's so beautiful there!

> Points: ——
> 8x1   8

6 Complete the sentences as in the example:

~~see the mountains~~	try their delicious burgers
invite all our friends	go snorkelling

A: We're going to take a helicopter ride.
B: Oh, good. We'*ll see the* ....
   .*mountains*............... , then!

1 A: We're going to go to the beach.
   B: Really? I ....
      .... , then!

2 A: We're going to have a party.
   B: Oh, good. We ....
      .... , then!

3 A: They're going to have a barbecue.
   B: Really? We ....
      .... , then!

> Points: ——
> 3x1   3

7 Write the questions. Use the words in brackets.

I don't want to wear a uniform at school. **(have to)**
Do I have to wear a uniform at ...
school?...............

1 I want to go to the cinema. **(may)**
   ....

2 I want to use your computer. **(can)**
   ....

3 I don't want to do my homework. **(have to)**
   ....

4 I want to visit my friend Jeff. **(can)**
   ....

5 I don't want to get up early. **(have to)**
   ....

6 I'll bring Emma an aspirin. **(shall)**
   ....

> Points: ——
> 6x2   12

8 **Choose the correct item.**

John .... a new bike yesterday.
A buying   **(B)** bought   **C** buys

1 Mother .... in the kitchen at the moment.
A cooks   **B** cooked   **C** is cooking

2 We .... to the cinema yesterday.
A are going   **B** went   **C** go

3 Tomorrow he ..... his grandmother.
A visit   **B** is going to visit
C visited

4 He .... football in the park yesterday.
A plays   **B** is playing   **C** played

5 They ..... dinner now.
A ate   **B** are eating   **C** eat

6 She ..... a letter at the moment.
A wrote   **B** is writing   **C** writes

7 I ..... my homework now.
A did   **B** do   **C** am doing

(Points: ——)
(7x2   14)

9 **Fill in *Where*, *Who*, *When*, *Why*, *What*, *How much*, *How many* or *Whose*.**

A: ..*Who*.. are you?
B: I'm Emma's brother.

1 A: .... is my bag?
B: On your bed.

2 A: .... is Peter?
B: In the bedroom.

3 A: ...... are you doing?
B: I'm washing the car.

4 A: ...... coat is this?
B: It's mine.

5 A: ...... are you crying?
B: I lost my dog.

6 A: .... is your music lesson?
B: At 8 o'clock.

7 A: .... apples do we need?
B: Seven.

8 A: .... is that man?
B: I think it's Peter.

9 A: .... bread do we need?
B: A loaf.

10 A: .... is the weather like?
B: It's rainy.

(Points: ——)
(10x1   10)

10 **Complete the text.**

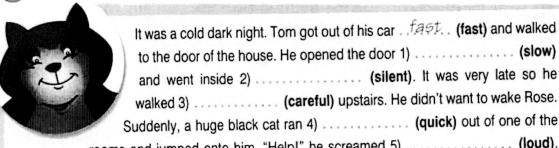

It was a cold dark night. Tom got out of his car ..*fast*.. **(fast)** and walked to the door of the house. He opened the door 1) .... **(slow)** and went inside 2) .... **(silent)**. It was very late so he walked 3) .... **(careful)** upstairs. He didn't want to wake Rose. Suddenly, a huge black cat ran 4) .... **(quick)** out of one of the rooms and jumped onto him. "Help!" he screamed 5) .... **(loud)**.
"It's OK," Rose answered 6) .... **(calm)**. "Meet Blackie. Our new pet cat!"

(Points: ——)
(6x2   12)

(Total: ——)
(100)

1 **Look at the picture and choose the correct item.**

This (is) / are a picture of my family. Look at 1) **our** / **us**! My parents 2) **is** / **are** called Fiona and Will. 3) **My** / **Me** mother is a pilot and my father is a doctor. Mark is my 4) **older** / **oldest** brother. 5) **Him** / **He** is standing behind my grandmother. My grandmother is sitting next to 6) **mine** / **me**. 7) **She** / **Her** name's Kelly. Rob, my 8) **younger** / **youngest** brother, is sitting with 9) **our** / **ours** grandparents. We are outside our house. 10) **It's** / **Its** in London.

Points: —— 10x1   10

2 **Fill in the gaps with *in*, *on* or *at*.**

I went to Greece .. *in* .. 2003.

1 We don't go to school ...... the weekend.

2 We'll meet ...... the evening.

3 It's cold in the Sahara ...... night.

4 I had a music lesson ...... Monday.

5 Schools aren't open .... New Year's Day.

6 You must come back ...... 11 o'clock.

7 My birthday is ...... July.

8 I play tennis ...... Saturdays.

Points: —— 8x1   8

3 **Look at the picture and number the phrases.**

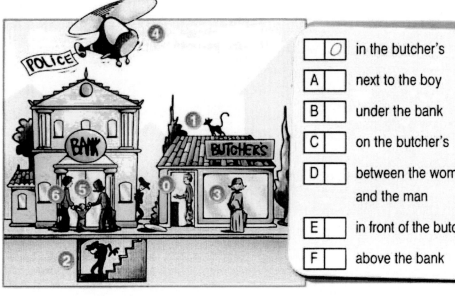

	O	in the butcher's
A		next to the boy
B		under the bank
C		on the butcher's
D		between the woman and the man
E		in front of the butcher's
F		above the bank

Points: —— 6x1   6

4 Write sentences.

(She's/beautiful/girl/I/know)   *She's the most beautiful girl I know.*

1 (He's/bad/at Maths/me)   ....

2 (I'm/careful/driver/in my family)   ....

3 (My car is/fast/yours)   ....

4 (It's/tall/tree/in the world)   ....

5 (I'm/old/you)   ....

> Points: ——
> 5x2   10

5 Underline the correct item.

I'm very tired! I think I **will go** / **am going to go** to bed early tonight.

1 "You're going to be late for work!" "I **will get** / **am going to get** a taxi."

2 I'm not sure but I think it **will snow** / **is going to snow** tomorrow.

3 "Your shirt is dirty." "I know. I **am going to wash** / **will wash** it today."

4 I **will buy** / **am going to buy** a suitcase today because I am going on holiday next week.

5 I'm not sure but I think Kim **will come** / **is going to come** to the school party.

> Points: ——
> 5x2   10

6 Read and match.

a	Do I have to have a visa to travel to England?
1	May I turn on the TV?
2	Shall I take you home?
3	Can I take my parrot with me?
4	Can I go now, Miss?
5	Shall I get you something to eat?

a No, you don't have to have a visa.

b Yes, you can. But you have to keep it in a cage.

c No, thanks. I'm not hungry.

d No, it's OK. I'll walk.

e Yes, but you mustn't forget to finish the exercise at home.

f Sorry, no. The baby is sleeping.

> Points: ——
> 5x2   10

7 Underline the correct question word.

A: <u>How</u> / Who are you?
B: Fine, thanks.

1 A: **Where** / **When** is the cat?
B: In the garden.

2 A: **What** / **When** is your birthday?
B: June 10th.

3 A: **What** / **Whose** radio is this?
B: Mary's.

4 A: **What** / **Why** nationality are you?
B: Italian.

5 A: **How** / **What** do you do?
B: I'm a nurse.

Points: ——
5x2   10

8 Choose the correct item.

You must talk **quiet** / (**quietly**) in the library.
1 Kurt is a **good** / **well** student.
2 "I love your present!" she said **happy** / **happily**.
3 My father gave me a **beautiful** / **beautifully** coat for my birthday.

4 Be **quiet** / **quietly**! I'm trying to think!
5 My brother always drives **careful** / **carefully**.
6 I ran **quick** / **quickly** into the house.
7 I was very **angry** / **angrily** with my little sister.
8 This is a **nice** / **nicely** scarf!

Points: ——
8x2   16

9 Choose the correct item.

Mother ...... the windows now.
A cleaned   (B) is cleaning
C is going to clean

1 I ...... my favourite cartoon yesterday.
A watched   B am going to watch
C watch

2 Ben ...... a book now.
A is reading   B reads   C read

3 I ...... a new CD tomorrow.
A buy   B bought
C am going to buy

4 He ...... his grandfather to the park yesterday.
A takes   B took
C is going to take

5 Listen! The birds ...... in the garden.
A sang   B are singing   C sing

6 The girl ...... to her mother now.
A is talking   B talks   C talked

7 When ...... to London? Was it last year?
A do you go   B are you going
C did you go

8 The film was long .... boring.
A because   B and   C or

9 You can visit me today .... tomorrow.
A or   B because   C but

10 I can't sing .... I can play the piano.
A or   B and   C but

Points: ——
10x2   20

Total: ——
100

157

Word List

A

above
action
address
adjective
adverb
affirmative
alligator
angry
animal
apartment
appetite
aspirin
autograph
awful

B

baked
baker's
bank
basket
beach
beard
bee
behind
below
bench
between
biology
bird
biscuit
blanket
boat
bone
boot
bored
boring
bottle
bowl
boxer
bracket
brick
brightly
brush
burger
burglary
bus stop
busy
butter
butterfly

C

camera
can
carrot
carton
cartoon
catch
celebrate

cereal
cheap
chicken
child
chocolate
circus
clap your hands
classroom
climb
clothes
clown
coat
coconut
cola
collect
command
compare
compose
concert
consonant
cook
countable
cousin
cup
cupboard
customer
cut

D

dangerous
decision
deer
definite
delicious
describe
dessert
diary
dictionary
difference
dig
dinner
dirty
disco
dish
drop
drum
dry
duck

E

electricity
email
empty
ending
Europe
evening
everywhere
evidence
excuse
expensive

expression

F

far
fast food
feed
feet
fence
fight
fish
flight
floor
flour
fly-fishing
foot
fork
form
fortune teller
fox
frequency
fridge
friendly
furniture
future

G

gently
get dressed
giraffe
give
glasses
goldfish
goose
grandfather
grandma
grass
greengrocer's
ground
grow
guest
guitar

H

habit
happen
hate
have to
helicopter
hill
hippo
hole
homework
honey
hoop
hospital
housework
hungry
hurry up
hurt

I

I'm starving
imperative
in
in front of
in the country
information
inside
instead
intention
interesting
interrogative
iron
item

J

jam
jar
joke
juice

K

keep off
kite
knife
knit
know

L

lady
lake
late
laugh
lay
lazy
leaf
leave
lemonade
liar
library
lie
lime
lion
live
lizard
loaf
lollipop
long
long form
look after
lorry
lose
loud music
lunch

M

magazine
main
make

manners
map
march
maths
may
mean
meat
medicine
memory
metal
midnight
mime
minute
mirror
miss
money
monkey
monster
month
moon
mop
morning
mosquito
motorbike
mountain
moustache
move
museum
must
my turn

N

near
necessary
necessity
need
negative
newspaper
next to
nod your head
noisy
noon
noun
number

O

object
obligation
obligatory
office
olive
on
onion
opposite
otherwise
outdoors
outside
own
ox

P

paint
paper
parent
past
pasta
path
people
permanent
permission
person
phone
photo
phrase
pick
pie
piece
pineapple
plan
planet
plant
plate
plenty
plural
poem
polite
politely
pond
possessive
possessive case
possibility
post
preposition
present
probably
programme
prohibition
pronoun
pumpkin
put

Q

quiet

R

reach
read
reason
relax
remain
report
restaurant
return
rhyme
ride a horse
ring
roller-skates
roof
row

rubber
rubbish
rude
rug
rule

S

sand
sandwich
scarf
scary
school subject
scream
seaside
send
sentence
serve
shall
share
sheep
shell
shine
short answer
short form
shout
shower
similar
skate
skirt
sky
sleep
slice
slide
slowly
snail
snake
snowball
snowman
someone
something
somewhere
soup
spelling
spider
spot
stamp your feet
stand
statue
stay
strawberry
street
subject
sugar
sweater
sweet shop
sweetie
swimsuit
swing
syllable

T

tail
take off
tasty
tea
theatre
thief
thirsty
throw
tidy
tiger
tired
toast
tomato
toothbrush
touch
traffic
tree-house
trick
tummy
turn (around)

U

uncountable
under
underwater
uniform
use

V

vegetable
verb
video camera
violin
visit
vowel

W

wall
wardrobe
warm
wash
watch TV
watermelon
wave your hands
weather
weekend
wheel
wild
winter
wood

Y

yacht
year

Z

zoo

Irregular Verbs

Present	Explain the verbs in your mother tongue.	Past	Explain the verbs in your mother tongue.
am / is / are	....	was / were	....
break	....	broke	....
bring	....	brought	....
buy	....	bought	....
catch	....	caught	....
come	....	came	....
cost	....	cost	....
cut	....	cut	....
do	....	did	....
draw	....	drew	....
drink	....	drank	....
drive	....	drove	....
eat	....	ate	....
feed	....	fed	....
find	....	found	....
fly	....	flew	....
forget	....	forgot	....
get	....	got	....
give	....	gave	....
go	....	went	....
have	....	had	....
hit	....	hit	....
hurt	....	hurt	....
keep	....	kept	....
learn	....	learnt / -ed	....
leave	....	left	....
lose	....	lost	....
make	....	made	....
meet	....	met	....
put	....	put	....
read	....	read	....
ride	....	rode	....
ring	....	rang	....
run	....	ran	....
see	....	saw	....
send	....	sent	....
sing	....	sang	....
sit	....	sat	....
sleep	....	slept	....
speak	....	spoke	....
spend	....	spent	....
swim	....	swam	....
take	....	took	....
teach	....	taught	....
tell	....	told	....
throw	....	threw	....
win	....	won	....
write	....	wrote	....